Notes from Father's Heart

Marvin Lynn Cantrell

◆◆◆◆◆◆◆

For my children:
Devotional notes from a father's
Daily prayer and Bible study

◆◆◆◆◆◆◆

(HBH)

Huckleberry Hill
Books

Published by
Huckleberry Hill Books
1291 Emory Road
Choudrant, LA 71227
www.huckleberryhillbooks.com

ISBN 978-0-9848398-0-3

With love and appreciation to Wanda,
my wonderful wife of thirty-eight years,
my editor and encourager,
whose support has made this book possible

In memory of my mother, Roberta, who led me to the
Lord and taught me from God's Word

CONTENTS

6

INTRODUCTION

This book began during my times of daily prayer and Bible study as I wrote notes in my prayer journal. It was in these times spent in God's presence that He opened scripture to me, answered my questions, and taught me lessons that were needful in my life. These journal notes later became devotional notes that I sent to my daughters in their young adult years. They took the form of short essays, poems, prayers that I had prayed, or thoughts about scripture I had read and contained illustrated truths that God had taught me. When I compiled this complete work for my children, I also included some other short inspirational pieces I had written over the years that expressed the values I wanted to pass on to them. At the urging of my children to publish the book, and after much prayer, editing, and re-writing, this devotional book has come to you.

Because this book came about during times of prayer, you will see prayers interspersed throughout the book. You will find my prayers in italics, and God's answers to prayers, as I perceived them, in bold italic quotes. Prayer is a personal conversation between you and God, and the only way to really learn prayer is to pray. It is my intent to encourage you to establish a regular practice of prayer every day; there is nothing more important in your walk with God than prayer and learning His Word.

This volume is divided into short segments, making it well-suited for devotional reading. It contains what I believe to be some of the most important themes in Christian life.

To my daughters, these pages were *"notes from father's heart."* It is my prayer that through these simple words you may receive **notes from your heavenly Father's heart**. Also, I pray that you will receive some insight that will be a blessing to you, help you live a godly life, and encourage you to spend time in His presence daily.

Marvin Lynn Cantrell

1
Keep Praying!
✞

I rise before the dawning of the morning,
And cry for help; I hope in Your word.
(Psalms 119:147)

I will be quiet and hear my God's thoughts;
They are not rushed, nor are they perishable;
His thoughts are eternal.
They bring peace to me.

The Sound of Life

Have you ever stopped and just listened? There is hardly any place you can go in this modern world without hearing the hum of man's machines. People find comfort in this hum; it means the ice is cold, dinner is warm, travel is easy, and entertainment is plentiful. The sounds of progress, the sounds of civilization, and the sounds of wealth being created—these all comfort and assure the modern man.

However, there is another sound that is not noisy and does not overpower. You cannot hear it unless you listen with your heart. It is the sound of His presence, His quiet, peaceful presence, which speaks to your soul. You must tune out all of man's engines and open an ear only to Him. He desires to speak to you and give you more comfort, strength, and joy in a moment than all those earthly machines can give you in a lifetime.

You must choose which sound you will hear. Choose to be busy and preoccupied with the hum of man's inventions, or draw aside and listen only to Him.

A daily discipline in your life must be to find that quiet place to hear the sound of life from the Giver of all life. It will not always be easy, nor will it always be hard, but you can rest assured, Jesus will always be there. It may seem that some days you hear only silence, and you get nothing from reading the Word. Keep listening; you will hear Him. Our God will never leave a truly hungry heart unfilled. In those silent days, He is only sharpening your listening skills. Keep listening, children; keep listening!

**To listen to His presence every day—
That is the engine of the soul.**

The Mind and Prayer

More than about making room in my schedule,
My prayer time is about making room in my mind;
I must make room for the presence of God.

A mind is a busy place,
One where we think, plan, dream,
Solve problems.
It is also the place where the soul
And the spirit commune with God.

My thoughts are like couriers
Bringing things to do and read.
I will tell all those busy thoughts to wait;
There will be time for them later.
Nevertheless, they scream, "This is important!
This thought is perishable and will never come again!"

What is most important?
If the great thought dies, cannot God raise it again?
Busy thoughts, rush on your way;
I will hear you another day.

I will be quiet and hear my God's thoughts;
They are not rushed, nor are they perishable;
His thoughts are eternal.
They bring peace to me.
In the quiet chambers of my mind,
I will make room for His presence.

Prayer without Confusion

How do I get rid of the confusion in my mind when I pray?
Lord, I really need an answer;
I want this confusion to be gone.
I yearn for an open heaven,
An unobstructed view of You.
You are the object of my desire.

Lord, let my worldly focus fade from view.
It is only You I want to see,
Not an inflated view of me.
My mind wanders, and my thoughts play tricks on me.
There is junk in the corridors of my mind.

O Holy Spirit, purify this house that is yours;
Sweep it clean of all that would hinder Your presence.
Wash out the stains of pride;
Sweep out the dust of neglect.

Burn away those rotting leaves of lust and corruption
That blow into the garden of my mind.
Make me a blank slate;
Inscribe on me anew
Only what pleases You.

Answer:
"Time is what it takes,
Unhurried and without regret;
Take time to focus your eyes on Me,
And tune your ears to heaven's symphony.

Come not like the prodigal before he went away,
Saying, 'Give me mine now;
I cannot wait.
I want everything my father has for me; I want it now.'

Come as the prodigal when he returned,
Saying, 'Father I just want to be in your house;
Please don't turn me away.
Anything you have for me is better than I have today.
I am not worthy, but I am willing to serve you.'

This returning prodigal came with nothing but himself;
He had no plans or agenda.
He only longed for a place to lay his head;
His desire was for food to satisfy his hunger.
Are you hungry, and tired of your own plan?

I have a plan for you;
A robe of righteousness,
A ring of authority,
Shoes for the rough path,
A feast in My house.
All your brothers are invited.

Leave all your own plans,
Those that took you to the hog pen afar.
Come to me, open and humble;
I will make you new,
And show you what to do."

Open a Channel of Prayer

> Confess your trespasses to one another, and pray for one
> another, that you may be healed. The effective, fervent
> prayer of a righteous man avails much. (James 5:16)

> Behold, the LORD's hand is not shortened, that it cannot
> save; nor His ear heavy, that it cannot hear. But your
> iniquities have separated you from your God; and your
> sins have hidden His face from you, so that He will not
> hear. (Isa. 59:1-2)

We need an open channel for the Lord to hear our
prayers; we must not allow sin to cut the heavenly phone
lines. Confess your sins when you pray, and as the Word says,
He is faithful and just to forgive. There is absolutely no doubt
that He will forgive, because the Word says He is faithful,
meaning He will not fail to forgive. (See 1John 1:9)

"Pray for one another" is a command, not a request. I
am always praying for you, my children; don't forget to pray
for me.

The term "righteous man" in this scripture is a problem
to some people, because they believe they are not good
enough to receive from God. The righteous man is so
because of Jesus Christ:

> For you are all sons of God through faith in Christ Jesus.
> For as many of you as were baptized into Christ have put
> on Christ. (Gal. 3:26-27)

Aren't you glad we don't have to depend on our goodness
to receive answers to our prayers from our righteous God?
We come to God clothed in the righteousness of Jesus Christ,
for there is no doubt that His righteousness pleases the
Father.

How Do I Worship?

Often, as I begin to pray I think of the example of prayer that Jesus gave His disciples. This prayer began with worship. I try to worship God, but my mind is rushing along to all the important things that need God's intervention. I try to think of some good worship words to voice to my God. When you think about it, this sounds more like trying to appease Him than worship Him. This worship falls flat and is powerless, no matter how good it may sound. It is a worship of worship, not a worship of God.

Lord, how do I worship You?

"Worship Me in spirit and truth." (See John 4:24)

How do I worship God in spirit and truth? First of all, it must come from deep in the heart—from the depth of the soul. My worship seems so shallow and so inadequate for my great God! How can a man pour forth worship that is worthy of the King of the universe? A man cannot give God worthy worship; he can only give true worship, and that is what God seeks. Worship cannot be made worthy in and of itself, but truth has worth because it is pure; thus, purity is the essence of the worship that God seeks. The worship that is worthy of my God is not always grand-sounding words and songs. True worship may not even be beautiful to the ear or sensible to the intellect. It is beautiful worship to my Lord because it is pure, and it is pure because it is truth. Truth makes no pretension and truth has no hidden agenda. Truth is what it is, pure and undefiled.

Worship God from the depth of the spirit with the undistorted and unpretentious truth that is there. Offer up to God what truly is in your heart, as feeble as it may seem, and He will magnify and multiply it, and cause it to bloom into a beautiful bouquet of worship to Him.

I Don't Know What to Say!

When I come to the Lord to pray,
Sometimes I don't know what to say.
I feel in awe of Him and not worthy to open my mouth.
I want to please God with my prayer,
But I don't know how to begin.
I may pattern my prayer after "The Lord's Prayer,"
And still I may find it hard to pray.

I am listening, and my spirit is reaching.
My thoughts wander;
I grab them like wayward children and
Tell them to sit down and be quiet.
I know I am in the presence of the Lord.

A part of me says, "Let's get on with it, Lord," but
I hear His gentle voice say, *"Sit still and be quiet."*
So, I wait expectantly.

After a while, I grow impatient.
I think I have something to say,
Petitions I want to bring.
Must we go so slowly?
Then my spirit says to my soul,
"Sit still and be quiet."
We need the Master.
Enjoy His presence; there is no hurry.
What more important thing do we have to do?

I worship Him as I wait; I tell Him of my love;
I feel His sweet embrace.
The channel is open now, and communion is on-going.
Now I can bring my petitions to Him,
But now I don't want to ask for things.

I just want to express my love for Him
And enjoy His presence!
The love of my God is sweet!
Now the tears are flowing and my heart is full.
I, a mere man, am in the presence of the King!

I feel a great urge to tell him all my failures of the last day
And ask His pardon.
I see in the spirit that His hand is raised;
He is motioning for me to be silent.
"It is covered by the Blood"!

I tell Him I love Him,
It comes from the depth of my being.
The Holy Spirit takes control and begins to pray for me;
He knows what I really need.

I have an audience with the King.
The door to His Holy of Holies is left open for me;
My access to Him is not at an end;
It is only at a pause, and I do not want to leave.

I look around like a janitor cleaning up after a meeting.
Seeing a few petitions stacked in a chair,
I walk over and hand them to Him,
Knowing all will be done well.
It is like an after-thought and of little consequence,
For the real business has already been transacted.
He says, *"Stay and talk a while, my friend."*

I look up into the sky after my prayer and say,
"I am happy with You, Lord."
I hear Him say with a smile in His voice,
"You had better be; I am all you have."
And I say, *"I don't want anything else."*

A Problem Blocks My Way

Lord, how do I get past my problem and find You? This problem looms so large, too high to see over, too wide to see around, and too heavy to lift up to You. I feel stuck, and don't know what to do. I know You can do anything, but why does it seem impossible to see past my problem? Is it my stubborn will which blocks the way before me and separates me from You? I want to yield to Your will so You can rebuild my world and make it function again according to Your plan. It is my plan that is the problem. My plan has failed, and I cannot salvage the pieces; they are broken beyond repair.

Lord, take the broken pieces and make something new. Show me what to do, for I have lost my way. My wisdom has failed me, but pride pushes me to keep trying to find a way to make my plan work. I cannot go another step without You, Lord. Show me how to start over, leaving my broken things behind and going forward into the perfect plan that I know You have for my life. Only You bring excellence and perfection; with You, all things work together for good. You can take the pieces of the most complex puzzle and put them together to make a beautiful picture. By Your Spirit, clear the fog that I might see the picture of what You want to do. By Your hand, put each piece of the puzzle in the right place to complete Your picture in my life. I know that You do all things well.

We all, from time to time, have prayed a prayer similar to this one, when problems loom so large that the light of the Son seems to be blotted out. Remember this: the Lord is your light, the Lord is your salvation, and the Lord is your strength. When you stand in His light, before long fear is washed away and His strength fills your life.

The LORD is my light and my salvation; whom shall I fear? The LORD is the strength of my life; of whom shall I be afraid? (Ps. 27:1)

Push the Day out of the Way

Lord, how do I push the day out of the way when I pray?
All the things I want to do—
All the things I need to do—
All the obligations I must keep—
I want to focus on you!

"Do you really want the day out of the way?
Am I more important to you?
Are you willing to let the day go its way without you?
Will the day be worse off without you?
Would you be worse off without Me?

Love Me more than the day,
And I will push the day out of the way.
The day can do without you,
But you cannot do without Me,
And I do not want to do without you.

Come, let us commune together,
Let the day go its way.
Later, I will provide you an hour
That will be of more value than all the day,
But the hour right now
Is the most valuable to Me and to thee!"

Through the Lord's mercies we are not consumed, because His compassions fail not. They are new every morning; great is Your faithfulness. "The LORD is my portion," says my soul, "Therefore I hope in Him!" The LORD is good to those who wait for Him, to the soul who seeks Him. It is good that one should hope and wait quietly for the salvation of the LORD. (Lam. 3:22-26)

The Wind in Our Sails

Keep running to God every day of your life; there is no other place to find strength. Without the strength of the Lord, we cannot go forward; we are only treading water or sinking. Without Him, our ship on the sea of life would drift aimlessly like a ghost ship, with all our weaknesses and sins exposed like old, dirty rags hanging limply from the masts; we are becalmed, with no wind of the Spirit to propel us onward.

As we come into the presence of the Lord and humble ourselves before Him, by His mercy all the grime we have collected along the way is washed away. There in His presence, fellowship with our Redeemer is renewed and we learn His way of truth. Now, when we hoist our sails, He blows powerfully into our sails and sends us forth in the power and joy of the Lord. We leave these times of prayer much strengthened and encouraged for the day ahead.

Remember that it is God, in His grace and mercy, who blesses us over and over again, filling our sails with wind, giving us power to go forth by His Spirit. At times, we find it so easy to begin to look at ourselves and think, "I must be good," or "I am a strong servant of God," or "I can do anything." It never is the "I." It is always God who is the power behind everything. When we let pride slip into our minds because of our own perceived goodness, we lose the wind again because of our own foolishness.

Since ancient times no one has heard, no ear has perceived, no eye has seen any God besides you, who acts on behalf of those who wait for him. (Isa. 64:4 NIV)

All of us have become like one who is unclean, and all our righteous acts are like filthy rags; we all shrivel up like a leaf, and like the wind our sins sweep us away. (Isa. 64:6 NIV)

Pray and Trust

> And when they ran out of wine, the mother of Jesus said
> to Him, "They have no wine." Jesus said to her, "Woman,
> what does your concern have to do with Me? My hour has
> not yet come." His mother said to the servants, "Whatever
> He says to you, do it." (John 2:3-5)

Mary simply made her concerns known to Jesus, and then
made a statement of faith. She did not worry about what He
would do or how He would do it. She gave it to Him; it was
now His concern, and no longer hers. She had neither the
ability to solve the problem nor the wisdom to know how it
should be solved, but Mary knew Jesus would provide what
was needed. In my mind, I picture Mary going back to the
celebration, no longer bothered about the wine.

We all have concerns that are better left with Jesus. Too
often, we bring our needs to Jesus and tell Him just how He
ought to handle them. Then, we are so busy looking for our
plan to be fulfilled that we may not even notice He has
already answered in another way. What seems to be a
problem only fades like the morning fog when the light of the
Lord shines on it.

Remember these very important things about prayer,
illustrated by Mary's simple request: bring your concerns to
Jesus and leave them there; trust Him to handle everything
for the good of His people.

It is enough to know that our concerns never need to
become worries; He will turn them into new wine.

Come and See

> Then Jesus turned, and seeing them following, said to
> them, "What do you seek?" They said to Him, "Rabbi"
> (which is to say, when translated, Teacher), "where are
> You staying?" He said to them, "Come and see." They
> came and saw where He was staying, and remained with
> Him that day (now it was about the tenth hour). (John
> 1:38-39)

"Where are You staying?" is such a simple question, but it
speaks volumes about the hearts of these seekers. They did
not say, "Come, stay at my house," or "Please come do
something for us." They wanted to go with Him. They said,
"You are our teacher; we want to go where You are going,
and do what You are doing." Jesus saw them following, and
asked them this question: "What do you seek?" Jesus gave
them an open door, and in no way limited what they could
ask of Him. They did not ask Him to get involved in their
plans, but they sought to get involved in His plan. Jesus did
not disappoint them. He said, "Come and see." They came to
the place where He was staying, saw what He was doing, and
remained in His presence.

Do our hearts yearn to hear Him say, "What do you
seek"? We have a very long list of things we seek and are
anxious to tell Him all about them. We want to know what is
going to happen to us and what great things He is going to
do; these guys just wanted to get involved in what Jesus was
doing and stay with Him.

Do we want to hear Jesus say to us, "Come and see"?
Time and again our prayers are frustrated because we are
seeking our own plans and not His. Seek His plan and His
purpose; there is no better life for you than following God's
plan. Listen for His voice every day when He says to you,
"Come and see."

Dry Times

There will be times when you will go through a dry season, feeling nothing when you pray. You may feel all alone and hungry for the presence of God. It may seem as if you have forgotten how to pray. You begin searching your life to find out what is wrong with you and where you went astray. If you look hard enough, you will find something ugly or questionable in your life. Confess it to God. It may still seem that your prayers are lifeless, and your spirit still longs for His presence. You may or may not find an answer for your drought.

Don't be afraid, and most of all, do not give up! God is always there; He always hears your prayers, even when it does not appear so to you. Remember it is never, ever a waste of time to pray. When the time is right, and you are desperate enough, you will find Him, and fellowship with your Lord will be as grand as ever.

Why do these dry times come in our prayer life? I do not have all the answers to this question, but I believe I have a little insight. Our faith in God is important; indeed, it is of the greatest value to Him. All things of great value must be tested and purified to prove their worth. To be sure, God knows all about our faith. He will show us who we are; then, He will show us who He is; the divide between the two will be vast. Nevertheless, God will reach across it and draw us to Himself because He desires for us to be in His presence. Even when you do not feel Him and have no sense of His presence, remember this: He is there by your side.

We love to have the grand and marvelous feelings in the presence of God, but feelings are like threads that are easily broken. Faith, on the other hand, is like a logging chain; it is faith that carries the load, and it will not break when the load is heavy. Even when we cannot see it, the power of God is on the other end of the chain.

Intercession

"Intercession: The act of intervening or mediating between differing parties; particularly the act of praying to God on behalf of another person."[1]

In chapter 25 of I Samuel, we see an illustration of intercession, with Abigail representing the intercessor, David representing God, and Nabal representing sinful man. Consider Abigail's intercession in the following verses:

> So she fell at his feet and said: "On me, my lord, on me let this iniquity be! And please let your maidservant speak in your ears, and hear the words of your maidservant." (1 Sam. 25:24)
> "Please forgive the trespass of your maidservant." (1 Sam. 25:28)
> Then she arose, bowed her face to the earth, and said, "Here is your maidservant, a servant to wash the feet of the servants of my lord." (1 Sam. 25:41)

Through Abigail, God teaches us much about intercession, what it is like and how it pleases God. We know from this scripture that Abigail was of good understanding and of beautiful appearance, and I believe that intercession is seen by God as beautiful and wise. She made haste when she heard of her husband's sin. She knew it would bring swift judgment. The intercessor must make haste and give God that for which He has already asked: the praises of his people. As Abigail did, the intercessor will humbly fall on his face before God and worship Him, taking the sin as if it was his own, and presenting the sin as it is, black and evil, without any honey coating. Declaring the righteousness of God's judgments and that sin deserves judgment, the intercessor pleads for forgiveness. Intercession brings blessing and great reward to the humble heart of an intercessor.

---

1. Trent C. Butler, Holman Bible Dictionary, (Holman Bible Publishers, 1991)

If You Ask

"If you ask anything in My name, I will do it." (John 14:14)

This simple, yet powerful verse sometimes seems too simple to accept. In this chapter, Jesus was teaching His disciples, followers of Jesus, imperfect people, just as we are imperfect people.

"If you ask," Jesus says, "I will do it." As I sit here looking back over my life at what I have asked Jesus to do for me, I cannot think of a time when He did not do for me what was needed, though not always just as I expected. I am sure that I have asked many things flippantly, carelessly, and selfishly; these prayers I soon forgot and the Lord knew I wasn't seriously asking. The word *ask* can also be translated *beg, crave, desire, or require.* We are asking for something that is very important to us, whether big or little in the eyes of others, and we will not forget about it.

Jesus goes straight to the heart of the prayer and what is really needed. Sometimes, you may pray about a very serious need in your life and think you know just what will satisfy that need. You look back later and see that He knew what was needed; He answered your prayer, though maybe not according to the way you thought. Other times, you may pray a very detailed prayer about what you desire, look back years later and see those details in reality. I was reminded of this very thing when I found a sheet of paper on which I had written, many years before, the details of some very important things we needed for our family. God provided abundantly. Jesus is so good to us. If you ask, He will do it.

The next thing Jesus said was, "If you love Me, keep My commandments" (John 14:15). **Will you do it?**

Wait

> But those who wait on the LORD shall renew their
> strength; they shall mount up with wings like eagles, they
> shall run and not be weary, they shall walk and not faint.
> (Isa. 40:31)

In this verse, we see that for a particular group of
people—those who wait—there are these benefits: renewing
of strength, soaring like eagles, and not getting weary. The
key is to wait and not be in a hurry; wait patiently on Him, for
He is worth the wait. What does it take to be one who waits
on the Lord? It must involve more than just being willing to
take the time. Many people use up great volumes of time in
the wait, and accomplish little. They are not those who are
running away from their troubles, or those who are avoiding
some distasteful task. Who are "those who wait"?

*Lord, teach me to wait. I already know how to waste time; I can do
that very well on my own. I want to wait expectantly, patiently, quietly
(not just a quiet mouth, but a quiet spirit) - with a heart full of desire.*

Desire may be the most important characteristic of
"those who wait," but what is the reason for the desire? Is it
so we can be strong, or soar with the eagles, or be that grand
person we always wanted to be? The desire is to kiss the face
of God, to bow at His feet, to be in His presence and
worship Him. That desire, in essence, is to fellowship with
my God and my Maker. Why did He make me in His own
image, except that I might fellowship with Him? He who
waits is not waiting for the strength or the soaring glory, but
for the embrace of his friend. Oh, to be one with Him!

> I wait for the LORD, my soul waits, and in His word I do
> hope. My soul waits for the Lord more than those who
> watch for the morning—yes, more than those who watch
> for the morning. (Ps. 130:5-6)

Some Reasons Prayers Are Not Answered

Rebellion: Sin against what God has shown you. "Your sins have hidden His face from you" (Isa. 59:2). Be a bond servant, not a rebel.

Unbelief: "But let him ask in faith, with no doubting, for he who doubts is like a wave of the sea driven and tossed by the wind. For let not that man suppose that he will receive anything from the Lord; he is a double-minded man, unstable in all his ways" (James 1:6-8). Have faith and do not doubt.

Not God's will: Accept God's way willingly.
"Now this is the confidence that we have in Him, that if we ask anything according to His will, He hears us" (1John 5:14). Have meekness, not stubbornness.

Selfish requests: "You ask and do not receive, because you ask amiss, that you may spend it on your pleasures" (James 4:3). His plan is the best plan.

Unforgiving heart: "And whenever you stand praying, if you have anything against anyone, forgive him, that your Father in heaven may also forgive you your trespasses" (Mark 11:25). Forgive and don't hold grudges.

Neglect of the Word: We must live by His Word. "One who turns away his ear from hearing the law, even his prayer is an abomination" (Prov. 28:9). Read and follow the instructions given by God.

Wrong relationship between husband and wife: "Wives, likewise, be submissive to your own husbands" (1Peter 3:1). "Husbands, likewise, dwell with them with understanding, giving honor to the wife, as to the weaker vessel, and as being heirs together of the grace of life, that your prayers may not be hindered" (1Peter 3:7). Work on reconciliation, because division is destructive.

Prayers Answered

How can I know my prayers will be answered? Though books could be written on the subject of answered prayer, I will strive to give a short answer. (I have already written on the previous page about the main reasons prayers are not answered.)

Answered prayer is all about God's Word. What He said, He will do. The Bible tells us how to pray, and Jesus even gave a model prayer in what we call "The Lord's Prayer." We try to put all sorts of extra criteria into receiving answers to our prayers, but it all boils down to what the Word says.

We put too much emphasis on ourselves when we pray. Our prayers are answered not because of our power with God, but because of His power, mercy, and love. We read scriptures such as, "If two of you agree on earth concerning anything that they ask, it will be done for them by My Father in heaven" (Matt. 18:19); then we pray for what we want and think that since we have agreed, now we will receive our answer. However, this agreement must be two souls praying in harmony with the Spirit of God and with each other, praying for what the three of us want, not just what the two of us want. Again, we must look to God and His Word.

One night at church someone asked for prayer according to the scripture, "Is anyone among you sick? Let him call for the elders of the church, and let them pray over him, anointing him with oil in the name of the Lord" (James 5:14). I did not go and pray with the others because I did not feel like praying at that moment, so I reasoned that others could be more effective praying for this person. Immediately, I heard the Spirit of the Lord say to me, *"It has nothing to do with you; it is My Word and I will honor My Word."*

Our part is to be His willing servants, completely yielded to His Word and to His plan in our lives, willing to accept the answer that He gives, whether or not it is pleasing to our flesh.

You may say, "How can I believe that any of my prayers will be answered? I am not a super-spiritual person or a great Bible scholar. I do not have any special place with God." You may not be an Elijah or a Paul, and there is probably more that you don't know about the Bible than you do know, but you do have a special place with God, and He does hear and answer your prayers. There will be an amazing change in your life when you understand that the God of the universe loves you! You are His precious one for whom He would move heaven and earth. You can enter into His presence and talk to Him right now!

Let me say it again: answered prayer is all about His Word. You can believe Him when He says He loves you and wants you to be one with Him. You can believe Him also when He says he wants you to keep His commandments. Jesus is the Word made flesh. You may or may not know the Bible in a scholarly way, but you must know the Word in a personal way and walk with Him in all the light He has given you.

> "That all of them may be one, Father, just as you are in me and I am in you. May they also be in us so that the world may believe that you have sent me. I have given them the glory that you gave me, that they may be one as we are one: I in them and you in me. May they be brought to complete unity to let the world know that you sent me and have loved them even as you have loved me." (John 17:21-23 NIV)

The Measure of Prayer

I find myself trying to measure the effectiveness of my prayers and begin asking myself these questions: Is my prayer measured by how many requests I have brought before my God? Is it determined by how I feel when I pray, or by the answers I see after I pray? Are my emotions the gauge of effective prayer, or is it my intellect that holds the measuring tape?

The Bible compares our relationship with the Lord to a marriage. How do I estimate the fruitfulness of intimacy with my wife? Do I gauge it by how much I have asked of her, or what she has given me? Does she measure the value of time with me the same way? No! Obviously, that would make us no more than users of each other. Ours is not a business relationship; it is a friendship, a love affair of the most valuable kind, the priceless kind. Why, then, do I find myself trying to measure my time with the Lord, how well I pray, or how much my prayers have accomplished?

What is prayer all about anyway? To know Him—that is the goal! The effectiveness of my prayer is not dependent on the number of important requests I have brought to Him, or even His answers to prayer. What makes prayer worthwhile is that intimate communion with Him, the fellowship with Him that I carry with me when I leave my time of prayer. There is no need to re-dial His number; the line is still open, and the fellowship continues.

In trying to appraise the value of my prayers, I evaluate only myself. No one can fully perceive the awesomeness of God and His love for us.

2
Be Encouraged
✞

"Because he loves me," says the LORD, "I will
rescue him; I will protect him, for he
acknowledges my name."
(Psalms 91:14 NIV)

Even to your old age and gray hairs I am he,
I am he who will sustain you.
I have made you and I will carry you;
I will sustain you and I will rescue you.
(Isaiah 46:4 NIV)

My Shepherd

As I sat one day pondering my problems and all the
seemingly endless impossibilities that life had put before me,
I felt prompted to read the twenty-third Psalm. In these six
powerful verses, I found a wealth of hope for my troubled
soul.

I would ask you, "Who is doing most everything in this
chapter?" It is the Lord who is shepherding His sheep and
bringing abundant blessings. He is their complete provision
as they follow Him. The sheep cannot provide for
themselves; they must depend totally on their shepherd. It is
God that brings us to the green and pleasant pastures in life
where we can rest and have our needs supplied. It is our good
Shepherd who calms the troubled waters before us, waters
that were raging rapids before we looked to Him. Daily our
souls need to be restored, and again it is the Lord that
restores what the struggles of life have drained out of us.
When we do not know which way to go, He leads us in the
righteous way because we are His and called by His name. It
is our awesome Shepherd that sets a feast before us. Even as
the enemy of the soul besieges us, God welcomes us into His
presence, with the anointing of a special guest.

Life no longer looked so impossible before me, for now I
saw that the Shepherd of my soul was leading me. There is
only one thing that I must do; I must walk fearlessly and
obediently through this deep, dark valley of life's troubles,
knowing He is with me. The rod of His Word and staff of
His Spirit give me great comfort as they prove He is present
with me.

As I follow Him farther, I see that my cup will not only
be full, but His blessings will overflow to others. (May they
spill over upon you, also.) In the beginning, I saw no
goodness or mercy, but now I see that goodness and mercy
are my constant companions as I follow my Shepherd to an
everlasting home in His presence.

You Don't Need Eyes to See

It is a cool spring morning. Across the yard, next to the woods, is a little bluebird house atop a pole. You don't need eyes to see when the mother bird flies to the door to feed her chicks; their chirping fills the morning air. Sometimes the mother bird flies to perch atop her house out of sight of the chicks and they are silent, not knowing she is very near.

My mind reflects upon the times I knew the Lord was near, when I felt his presence, when I cried out to Him for the food only He could provide. Other times, I had no sense of His presence; I felt blind to His light and I longed for it to shine in my dark path again.

As I sit with my eyes closed, I know by the chirping when the little bluebird has perched in the birdhouse door. I hear the Spirit speaking to me, *"You don't need eyes to see that I am near; I am with you always even to the end of the world."*

Fear begins to wrap its dark fingers around us when we feel alone on the dark path, not being able to see a secure future before us, not knowing if all will be well in our tomorrow. Then is the time to trust Him. He is always present in the tomorrow building a secure today before we arrive.

As I look up, I see the little mother bird perched on a fence post, keeping watch over her nest from thirty feet away. God is near, keeping watch over me even if I don't see Him, so I will listen with the ears of faith to the sound of His still small voice, *"I am here with you; do not fear; I will bring what you need and what your soul desires. You don't need eyes to see that I Am."*

Struggles: Situation Normal

One day I lay on my bed and prayed, or more accurately, complained, *"I am tired of struggling."* It seems that there is always some kind of struggle in my life, with myself, with money, with people, with making the right decisions, and on and on.

As soon as I said my little five word prayer, God answered me powerfully: *"Think of all the people in the Bible. Were any of them without struggles? Did any of them come to a place where they no longer had struggles? Look at Abraham: He struggled with his neighbors wanting to take his wife; he struggled to receive the child of promise, Isaac, and then to raise the knife to kill him. Think of Moses who had struggles with himself, with the Egyptians, and with the Israelites. Think of David: He struggled with the lion and the bear, with Saul, with his own lust, and with his wayward sons. Think of Elijah, Paul, and all the prophets and apostles. Did any of them not struggle all the days of their lives?*

On the other hand, think how each of them was given a name: Abraham, "Father of Nations"; Moses, "Law Giver" and "Friend of God"; David, "A Man after God's Own Heart"; Elijah, "Prophet of God"; Paul, "Apostle to the Gentiles." Also, each of them was blessed and given a promise: Abraham was promised the land over which he walked; Moses was promised that God would go with him; David was promised his sons would sit on the throne of Israel (Jesus, the Son of David, will sit on the throne forever)*; Elijah did not have to pass through death, but went directly to the presence of God in the whirlwind; Paul was promised a reward in heaven."*

I heard these last words in my spirit from my God very clearly, *"The struggles will not go away, but neither will my blessings."*

Struggles Prepare the Heart

Do we get what God wants for us by struggling for it? Of what value are all the struggles we go through on the way to God's promise (struggles with ourselves, with faith, or should I say, the lack of faith)?

We may think of life's battles in the way a farmer prepares his field to be planted. The amount of work it takes to prepare the ground to be planted depends on the condition of the field. If the field has only a little grass, there may only need to be a thorough plowing. On the other hand, if the field is overgrown with trees, there is much more work to be done. The trees must be cut and the stumps removed; then the field must be plowed and the tree roots gathered up and burned. In either case, the seed has not yet been planted or a harvest reaped. The farmer's work only prepared the field.

We may wrestle with our past, our present, or our future, but in the end, our struggles do not get us God's promises. They only get us ready to receive His promises and wonderful gifts. We do not buy from God, nor do we pay for His blessings with our great effort. His gifts are free and come in His time, always on time, sometimes just in time.

I look at all the good gifts that God has given me throughout my life and cannot remember there ever being a struggle for them. Oh, I prayed and clung to faith, but I did not have to make things happen or force circumstances to come out for my good. Most of the time, God just dropped His gift into my hands in the most surprising way, when I least expected it.

We do not struggle to receive God's blessing or even to accomplish anything of consequence. Our struggles prepare the heart for God to do in us what is pleasing to Him and for the benefit of His kingdom.

High Praise

For we do not wrestle against flesh and blood, but against principalities, against powers, against the rulers of the darkness of this age, against spiritual hosts of wickedness in the heavenly places. (Eph. 6:12)

We do a lot of wrestling in our minds with real and imagined problems. All sorts of things come against us to steal our peace and destroy our fellowship with God. These powers try to rip our faith from us. On numerous occasions in my life, I have been hit with a frustrating problem, and then another, and another, and another, until the weight of these problems seemed unbearable. The temptation was to become angry, wrestle the problems, and become depressed, doubting that God even cared. Our enemy knows our weaknesses and will offer to us a pleasing sin to console us, or will bring to our minds numerous reasons to doubt God.

Stop looking down and start looking up; lift up your voice; it is time to praise our King. There is power in praise because it turns our focus from our problems to our Savior. It is easy to think we have everything under control, but in reality, God is in control. Our salvation is in God, always has been, and always will be. When we praise Him, He takes the fight to the enemy and prevails. Psalms 149 pictures this battle splendidly. Our praise is like a double-edged sword that slices through doubt, chops away fear, and destroys all our enemies, real or imagined.

The LORD takes pleasure in His people; He will beautify the humble with salvation. Let the saints be joyful in glory; let them sing aloud on their beds. Let the high praises of God be in their mouth, and a two-edged sword in their hand, to execute vengeance on the nations, and punishments on the peoples; to bind their kings with chains, and their nobles with fetters of iron. (Ps. 149:4-8)

Feed on His Faithfulness

> Trust in the LORD, and do good; dwell in the land, and
> feed on His faithfulness. (Ps. 37:3)
> (Read all of chapter 37)

What is this bread of faithfulness that will nourish our souls?

First, we must understand what faithfulness is. It is immovable and never changing; it is always there, always dependable; it is not going to go away. It is as solid as a rock; it is the foundation stone on which to build a life. Our bodies feed on perishable food, but our eternal souls must feed on the imperishable. As the old saying goes, "You are what you eat." If the soul feeds on the perishable it will perish, but if the soul feeds on the eternal, then it will live in the eternal.

We must not only affirm with the mind His faithfulness, we must make it the foundation of our lives, depending on its nourishment to give us life. We must put ourselves on an exclusive diet of depending on Him alone to give us every single spiritual vitamin that is needed for our souls. Do we hunger for God and what He wants to provide for us or for the constant entertainment, excitement, and thrills the world uses to tantalize us? Throw away the toxic "junk food" of the world; there is no life in it. Delight in the Lord; He will bring your righteousness to light, and cause your integrity to be plainly seen.

Feed on His faithfulness and your inheritance will be forever. He will be your strength in troubled times because you have put your trust only in Him.

The Treasure Within

> We have this treasure in earthen vessels, that the
> excellence of the power may be of God and not of us.
> (2 Cor. 4:7)

"This treasure" is the Gospel which enlightens to us the glory of God. Freely given to the entire world, this glorious Gospel, the light of God, is able to bring salvation when it shines into the darkness of the heart. Jesus is our salvation and our reconciliation to fellowship with God. He is the Word written on the pages of our hearts, and He is the strength of our lives.

We are but vessels of earthly substance through which God has chosen to work. By our words and by our lives, the light of His presence shines out radiantly from these clay pots to a world greatly in need of His love. It is His power that makes us able to prevail in whatever circumstance we find ourselves. He is the one who speaks through us to the world and who brings about change in the hearts and lives of men. The glory of the awesome Gospel is manifested in our weakness so that it is clearly seen as Jesus in us, not we ourselves.

In this chapter, Paul was saying to the church that he was preaching the Gospel with his life, even through hardship and suffering. We are always dying to ourselves, just as Jesus died to self, so that when people look at us, they will see the life of Christ in our frail flesh.

We do not possess this treasure; the treasure possesses us. It is liberating to understand that we do not need to desperately grasp at anything, but just to be His willing vessel; all that is needed will be provided. Do not strive to be strong, but be willing to be weak that Jesus may be strong in you.

Temporary

> Therefore we do not lose heart. Even though our outward man is perishing, yet the inward man is being renewed day by day. For our light affliction, which is but for a moment, is working for us a far more exceeding and eternal weight of glory, while we do not look at the things which are seen, but at the things which are not seen. For the things which are seen are temporary, but the things which are not seen are eternal. (2 Cor. 4:16-18)

This life that we live on the earth today is only temporary; it will pass. I remember one time about thirty-five years ago I was complaining about something on my job. I have long since forgotten what the problem was, but I remember clearly what a co-worker said to me: "I can go through almost anything if I know it is only going to be for a short time."

Jesus Himself has said, "I will never leave you nor forsake you" (Heb 13:5). What He has chosen to do through you, He will do by His power, so don't lose heart. What today may look like a big problem will tomorrow look like nothing when we see that the Master's hand has always been at work. He is working on something much bigger than you can imagine in your life and in those you befriend. No, you can't see it now; maybe you can't even dream of it now, but the unseen power of the Eternal One is at work in your life. Don't doubt His plan, don't doubt His purpose, and never, ever doubt His power to do great and marvelous things through you, things that may not be known to you until you receive your reward as a faithful servant.

We live and view our lives today in the temporary, but God always sees and works in the eternal. Our trials are temporary, but what our Lord is doing in us is eternal. To be sure, God always does all things well!

Rescue

"Even to your old age and gray hairs I am he, I am he who will sustain you. I have made you and I will carry you; I will sustain you and I will rescue you." (Isa. 46:4 NIV)

How many times I have called to my Lord, "Help me! I have lost my way again!"

My God is all about rescue; that is what He does. He opened the Red Sea to rescue His children. He sent young David to slay a giant and rescue an army, sent an angel to slay an army of 185,000 men in order to save a city (see 2 Kings 19:35), sent ravens to feed His servant Elijah, and sent an earthquake to deliver Paul and Silas from prison. Most importantly, He sent His Son to pay the price with His blood to rescue us from hell.

We must never doubt His love for us! He will come after us when we stray, never hesitating to leave the ninety-nine in the sheep fold and go after that one lost lamb. Often that lost sheep was me or you, when some glitter caught our eyes and we wandered off from the green pastures of fellowship with Him. We got too busy to pray and neglected the lover of our hearts.

He desires our fellowship as much as we need Him for our very existence. He loves us so much that He will move heaven and earth to rescue us. Never think you have wandered so far that you are out of His reach; never believe the lie from hell that says, "God doesn't care about you." He will rescue—that is what He does. We only have to reach, and He will reach farther. We only have to call, and we will hear His voice echoing through all the earth, *"Here I am at your side."* He is a lover pursuing His beloved.

"Because he has set his love upon Me, therefore I will deliver him; I will set him on high, because he has known My name." (Ps. 91:14)

Anchor of Hope

Because God wanted to make the unchanging nature of his purpose very clear to the heirs of what was promised, he confirmed it with an oath. God did this so that, by two unchangeable things in which it is impossible for God to lie, we who have fled to take hold of the hope offered to us may be greatly encouraged. We have this hope as an anchor for the soul, firm and secure. It enters the inner sanctuary behind the curtain, where Jesus, who went before us, has entered on our behalf. He has become a high priest forever, in the order of Melchizedek. (Heb. 6:17-20 NIV)

An anchor causes a ship to stay secure and unmoved in the spot the captain chooses. We have an anchor for the soul; it is not made of metal that can rust away with time, nor is it anchored in the sands of the sea floor. Because of the oath of God, we can be sure our anchor will never fail to hold us.

We cannot serve God if we have no hope of salvation. God created the need for hope within us; He will fulfill our expectation and will never leave us hopeless. Though we may sometimes feel tossed about by life, we can check our anchor and be assured that it will always hold. The only way our anchor can ever be removed is if we, by our own will, choose to cut our anchor cable and trust in our own resources. Let us always choose to run to Him, the one in whom we will find hope that is always secure. There is no hope apart from God.

Thank You blessed Savior for making it so abundantly clear, over and over again, that You are our hope, and that your desire is for us to place our trust in You, knowing that You will never, ever leave us hopeless.

Rest

Rest in the LORD, and wait patiently for Him. (Ps. 37:7)

I will feed My flock, and I will make them lie down," says the Lord GOD. (Ezek. 34:15)

"Come to Me, all you who labor and are heavy laden, and I will give you rest. Take My yoke upon you and learn from Me, for I am gentle and lowly in heart, and you will find rest for your souls." (Matt. 11:28-29)

Rest has different shades of meaning in these four verses, but it all comes down to faith and peace. The message in Psalm 37:7 is, "Calm down, child, I've got everything under control." We get so upset when things don't go just as we have planned, but if we stop to think, we realize that we control very few things, anyway. I'm so glad He controls all things; otherwise, I would be in a big mess. We spend far too much of our lives in a state of turmoil for no good reason. God has everything under control and always will, so just rest in Him.

The Lord is saying in Ezekiel 34:15 "I have a place for you to rest peacefully." We must believe it is God's will for us to be at rest spiritually, even while we are busy about our daily lives. We must also take some time to rest the body and mind.

Sometimes we don't experience the rest He has promised because we will not follow His leading. Jesus says, "Come to Me; I have a rest for you." He gives a prerequisite to finding rest, and that is being yoked up to the load with Him. After a while we start to walk in step with Him, act and talk like Him. Do you think Jesus ever, ever worries about the load or gets bothered by the load? No, Never! So learn from Him and find rest for your souls.

Pure Water

This morning I began to think of a barren place with no pure, fresh water—only salt water. Then I began to envision a tent still, with which to make fresh water from salt water. The still is made by placing a clear, plastic covering with the center formed into the shape of a cone (point down) over a pan of salt water. An empty vessel is positioned in the pan under the point of the cone. The still is then placed in the sun. As the sun shines through the covering, water vapor begins to collect as droplets on the bottom of the plastic and runs down to the point of the cone and into the vessel that receives the pure water.

My life is the salt water, and as Jesus shines upon me, I am changed and reformed one drop at a time by His Spirit. The drops come together and run down the finger of the Holy Spirit, dripping into this earthen vessel, which as time passes becomes full and overflows with pure water. The more the light of the Son shines on me and exposes me before Him, the more pure water comes forth. I must be continually and completely covered by His Spirit (the clear plastic) for this process to work as it should. If the tent of the Holy Spirit does not completely cover me, the winds will blow away the vapor before it has time to be transformed; impurities or desert sand will enter and pollute the water; then it must be distilled all over again to be of any use.

The full vessel is emptied out and refilled continually as a life of usefulness for the kingdom of God.

Lord, help me to lay bare before you all of myself, to seek You continually in prayer and Bible study, that Your living Word might shine on me and purify me for your purposes. Never stop baptizing me totally and completely in your Holy Spirit; let me not be polluted by this world. Teach me, Lord, to be always open before You—to hear You—to obey You—to be useful in Your kingdom.

No Condemnation

Every Christian who has ever lived has, at one time or another, felt condemned. Condemnation is one of the most effective traps used by our adversary, Satan, to destroy us. The trap works like this: Satan whispers in your ear, "You have sinned and failed God, and you know what the Bible says about sin. You have broken God's law, not just once, but repeatedly. It is no use trying to follow God; give it up; it is hopeless. You are going to sin, anyway; just forget God and enjoy sin's pleasures."

"There is therefore now no condemnation to those who are in Christ Jesus, who do not walk according to the flesh, but according to the Spirit" (Rom 8:1). This "no condemnation" is not to those who are perfect, who have never sinned, but those who walk according to the Spirit. "For the law of the Spirit of life in Christ Jesus has made me free from the law of sin and death" (Rom. 8:2). As long as we keep following the road to heaven, we are walking according to the Spirit. Occasionally, we are going to slip and fall. Jesus has already paid the price for our redemption, and He is ready and willing to reach farther than we can imagine, delivering us from our own foul-ups. Just think what He has already done for us on the cross before we even knew Him. Would He do any less for us now, as we endeavor to follow Him?

To whom will we listen? The kind and gentle Holy Spirit says, ***"Reach out to Jesus who is faithful and just to forgive."*** Satan, the father of lies, says, "God doesn't care about you because you are a loser, always falling back into sin and messing up your life. Why would He continue to waste His time with you?" Can you imagine a parent refusing to help his little child when he falls down and cries out for help? How much more can we depend on Jesus who said, "I will never leave you or forsake you." (See also I John 1:9 and I John 2:1-2.)

Times of Temptation

The enemy of the soul is not always present, but he will come time and again to tempt us. When we are at a weak point, tired, or too busy, temptations may seem to be much stronger than usual.

He will cause your mind to seem saturated with evil thoughts and desires, and because of this, you may feel as if your mind has fallen into hell. The enemy will then say to you, "It is in your heart. Why not enjoy the fruit and indulge in the sin you know you desire?" It is at this point that you may fall prey to the temptation, rationalizing and agreeing with the lies of the enemy.

When this happens to you, call for help from Jesus! The enemy will say, "God will not hear you with all that evil in your heart." The carnal man in you will say, "Do not call on Jesus right now; He will help you overcome temptation, and this thing is too inviting." Don't listen to the enemy or the carnal man! Call on Jesus; He will hear you! The Lord may not always take away the temptation, but will give you the courage to choose to stand with Him in His power. You will be able to say, "Be gone from me in the name of Jesus, for I stand with Him." Then you will see a change in your mind and spirit.

You may not have won the battles with temptations in the past, but you can win the battle now. God's power is there for you, if you will only ask! He is waiting expectantly for your call. This seems much too simple, but it actually is this simple. We are tricked by our own minds and by the enemy into believing that there is no way to walk away from sin. The truth is that we can overcome temptation when walking hand in hand with Jesus.

What Is Perfection?

We have in our minds' eyes a picture of perfection, yet in reality, the image we have in our minds is almost never duplicated in real life. When we let our happiness be controlled by the picture of perfection in our minds, we will find that happiness eludes us, because reality never quite equals the dream. Do I throw away the dream in my mind, or let it be subdued by the flaws of reality? I will soak my mind in God's Word; then, when life does not turn out as I dreamed, I will see it in the light of God's love and faithfulness.

Life feels perfect as I sit here in the cool breeze of the morning, listening to the birds calling to their fellows and watching the sun rise behind the trees, while the little white, fluffy clouds float away. Life goes on, however, and this moment will pass; the rough edges of life will soon intrude into this perfect world. Even though my dreams for my life are not developing as planned in the perfect world of my thoughts, God has everything perfectly in control in the real world, and He will cause all things to work together for good to them that love and follow after Him with a true heart.

> Every good and perfect gift is from above, coming down from the Father of the heavenly lights, who does not change like shifting shadows. He chose to give us birth through the word of truth, that we might be a kind of firstfruits of all he created. (James 1:17-18 NIV)

Perfection for a man is, in its essence, living in perfect union and oneness with his God.

Thank You, Lord, for the good and perfect gifts that you give me every day. Let my life be offered up as firstfruits to You.

3
Grace Waits for You
✝

"So now, brethren, I commend you to God and to the word of His grace, which is able to build you up and give you an inheritance among all those who are sanctified." (Acts 20:32)

God gives His grace to us freely, but He does not force it on us. When we come to the end of ourselves and look up, He is there with an abundant supply of grace.

Grace Is Sufficient

What is Grace? "Grace bestows Christ's merit and Christ's standing forever." "Any intermixture of human merit violates grace. God's grace thus provides not only salvation but safety and preservation for the saved one, despite his imperfections."[1]

How do I receive grace? God gives His grace to us freely, but He does not force it on us. When we come to the end of ourselves and look up, He is there with an abundant supply of grace.

> Not that we are sufficient of ourselves to think of anything as being from ourselves, but our sufficiency is from God. (2 Cor. 3:5)

God's grace is always exactly enough. It is sufficient to save us and to keep us throughout life's journey. Sometimes I get a little concerned when I cut things too close; I want to be there early, have extra money to cover any cost, have more than enough time, and know every detail in advance. When we are in the Lord's boat of grace, it may look as if the boat could sink anytime, but it never does. On the tempest-tossed sea, the disciples cried in terror, "Lord, save us! We are perishing!" (Matt. 8:25). Jesus calmed the sea, and the waves did not cover them. We are always struggling to have extra in every aspect of life, forgetting that it is not the extra that delivers us from trouble and need, but the grace of God that makes the little to be just enough. When the temptation comes (and too often it will) to leave prayer and the Word and run to the work that must be done, stop and remember that our sufficiency is from God; everything we need is supplied in His grace.

---

1. Merrill F. Unger, *Unger's Bible Dictionary*, (Moody Press., 1966), 430.

From Faith to Grace

> Therefore, having been justified by faith, we have peace
> with God through our Lord Jesus Christ, through whom
> also we have access by faith into this grace in which we
> stand, and rejoice in hope of the glory of God.
> (Rom. 5:1-2)

Faith is the channel we have opened through which
justification can move. This justification is accomplished
because our Savior paid the price for the sin that is charged
against us; therefore, God's judgment in our case is acquittal;
His declaration is that we are made righteous (just as if we
never committed any sin). We have peace with Him through
Jesus, the source of our justification and the door of *access* to
His *grace*.

By God's grace we have legal standing that gives us the
privilege to be adopted into the family of God. Our position
as a child of God brings about a *regeneration* (re-creation or
new birth); because of this, we are able to rejoice in *hope* of
the glory of God.

Justification brings to us the robe of *righteousness* (peace
with God because of His Son's blood). In the realm of grace,
there is no time lapse between faith and standing in
righteousness before God. Our sanctification, which is
holiness or consecration to God, is immediate.

Faith gives *justification* and *sanctification* a road on which to
travel. When we accept the salvation God offers to us by
placing our faith in Jesus, we are covered by His Blood; we
are instantly made righteous and holy in His sight. As we walk
with God through this life to our future of eternal bodily
presence with our Savior, the Holy Spirit continues to
sanctify (refine and purify) us. Rejoice always in His grace
which is sufficient for your complete and eternal salvation.

From Tribulation to Hope

> But we also glory in tribulations, knowing that tribulation
> produces perseverance; and perseverance, character; and
> character, hope. Now hope does not disappoint, because
> the love of God has been poured out in our hearts by the
> Holy Spirit who was given to us. (Rom. 5:3-5)

In God's grace, we are able to glory in tribulation because
by faith we understand that tribulation produces in our lives
an endurance that will stand the test of time. By faith, we can
grasp the knowledge that we stand righteous in His realm of
grace, and we can be sure that anything that causes us to
focus on Him for strength will give us perseverance and will
make us strong in character. We can be steadfast in the truth,
unchangeable no matter the circumstance, knowing who we
are and where we stand (in His grace).

How does character produce hope? The man of character
will still be standing when lesser men have run away in fear.
This man who has stood his ground on the road of faith can
be sure his standing is in grace, because faith is eternally
connected to grace, and in the realm of grace, hope is as the
air we breathe. This hope never disappoints us, because when
we stand in God's realm of grace, it is the channel through
which He pours His love into our hearts. If hope is as a
breath of air, then the Holy Spirit is the oxygen in the air, the
energizing force in our spirits and the reality of God in us.

> You also were included in Christ when you heard the word
> of truth, the gospel of your salvation. Having believed, you
> were marked in him with a seal, the promised Holy Spirit,
> who is a deposit guaranteeing our inheritance until the
> redemption of those who are God's possession—to the
> praise of his glory. (Eph. 1:13-14 NIV)

From Death to Life

One man caught a deadly disease which spread to all mankind; thus death reined over the human race. There was a temporarily effective cure, but so much treatment was required that no one could endure it continuously.

Another Man came proclaiming, "There is a cure to humanity's deadly plague; it is in My flesh." The great doctors of the world said to Him, "If all our treatments cannot cure this deadly disease, what can one man like you do?" They had Him arrested as a fraud. The leaders of the land and the great doctors feared He would turn the people from their dependence on those who dispensed the medicine (the law), thereby causing them to lose their power over the people.

He was tried and convicted on trumped-up charges. His accusers executed Him by nailing Him to a tree, and as His blood flowed to the ground, a strange thing happened. As it dripped to the ground, it began to spread over everything—over the people and over the city—until it covered all of mankind.

Those who had heard and believed His words (which the authorities had called fraudulent) were thankful for the blood; it was the cure, just as He had said. Those who accepted the cure no longer died, but lived with health and strength.

Alas! Most people could not believe that this blood could bring a cure, and for them it did not, because the disease was in their hearts and minds. The men that believed were cured, and those that did not believe were not cured.

The disease was sin, and the law could not cure it. This Sinless Man who brought the cure had known all along that the only way for men to be free from the dreadful disease was for Him to give His Life, His Blood. This gift was given to us by Jesus, our Creator. He now waits for us to receive His free gift and come to Him in the realm of grace.

Grace Restricted

We then, as workers together with Him also plead with
you not to receive the grace of God in vain. (2 Cor. 6:1)

"You are restricted by your own affections" (2 Cor. 6:12).
This statement, with emphasis on the word affections, struck
me as key to grace. Where do I place my affections? What
things do I like? How do I like to spend my time? Where do I
like to go? Have my affections for the world blocked His
grace?

Grace is not stopped by my affections; it is always
plentiful in supply. Even so, am I receiving grace in vain?
Grace is there, ready and on call, but I'm not calling. I am
looking the other way, down the road to the objects of my
affections. Would you dare try to drive a car down the road
with your eyes closed? No—of course not! Neither can you
navigate down the road of spiritual life with your eyes fixed
anywhere but on Jesus. Certainly, you can enjoy the scenery
along the roadside and enjoy life as you go, but don't let your
eyes stray too long from the road of grace. Jesus is the narrow
way, the only way to true joy and all the good things in life,
even to life itself.

Grace can be restricted only by you and the choices you
make. Keep the eyes of your heart stayed on the Master and
you will forever be surrounded by His grace.

Grace Is Waiting

There are good words in my mind, but they are hidden deep under the piles and piles of junk and rubbish. I want to sweep the rubbish out of my mind so the good words that are hidden there can see the light of day.

From where do grace and inspiration come, except from the Spirit of God? He is the Spirit of grace. Is the Spirit buried under this pile of junk in my mind? Do I cover Him over with all the foolishness that passes for good in the world, all that claims to be great and enjoyable, all that claims to be profound and indispensable? True greatness can be buried under that stack of worthlessness. He (the Spirit) desires to speak, but I stick a sock of entertainment in his mouth. His wisdom is hidden behind my smoke screen of chatter. I suppress His words under a blanket of activity. I unconsciously think that I must be continually busy, thus leaving no time for something truly great and good to come forth. Why, oh why, must I countless times repeat my foolish actions, without even thinking what I am doing?

Stop! Give Him voice! Be quiet! Listen! He has a loving word that will salve the hurt. He has a heavenly smile that will fill you with joy. He has more to give than we have room to hold. His inspiration and wisdom will give us what is needed to meet and to conquer the day. His peace will satisfy us in the night seasons.

God is the author of the greatest of masterpieces: *grace*. It is there for us in the depth of the Spirit; if we will open the gates and let it flow, God's grace will fill us to overflowing.

The Stain

When is the best time to get a stain out of your clothes? As you may already know, the sooner the stain is removed, the better the chance it will not remain. Get the stain out now. If you wait, the stain will become set in the cloth and will only be harder to remove.

The stain of sin in your life is the same way; it is best to get the stain out right away. The longer sin's stain stays in your life, the harder it will be to remove; it only grows and gets deeper. Don't wait until later, when you think you will be stronger or wiser; bring it to God now and let Him wash you clean. The longer you wait, the worse the permanent stain will be in your life.

The first thought that usually will come to mind is, "It cannot be that easy; after all, I have sinned before God!" If you are truly sorry for your sin and come to God in repentance, he will forgive. God's grace is always bigger than the power of any sin! I cannot promise you that there will be no trace of your sin left behind in the fabric of your life on earth, but because of His forgiveness the stain of your sin will not condemn you before God. Grace is waiting for you, but you must take the first step.

> If we confess our sins, He is faithful and just to forgive us our sins and to cleanse us from all unrighteousness. (1 John 1:9)

It was so liberating to me to understand this one principle: The hand of the Lord is stretched out to us when we sin; He is just waiting for us to reach up, take His hand, and be forgiven. We do not have a mandatory period of time to suffer for our sin before we can ask for forgiveness. My Jesus does not stand over me with a sword to cut me down when I fall; He extends a strong arm to lift me up.

This wonderful grace and mercy of God is a remedy for sin, but it is not a license to sin, and must never be used by man to live any way he pleases. God always knows the desires of the heart.

Those who live according to the sinful nature have their minds set on what that nature desires; but those who live in accordance with the Spirit have their minds set on what the Spirit desires. (Rom. 8:5 NIV)

God has a river of mercy flowing. We live in a sinful world, and when we get contaminated by sin in our daily walk, we can step into the river and let it wash us as white as snow. This endless river of mercy endures forever.

Grace's Fragrance

> Now thanks be to God who always leads us in triumph in
> Christ, and through us diffuses the fragrance of His
> knowledge in every place. For we are to God the fragrance
> of Christ among those who are being saved and among
> those who are perishing. (2 Cor. 2:14-15)

Our lives are like a perfume bottle which God has filled
with the aroma of His grace. This sweet smell of the fragrant
knowledge of Christ poured out of our bottles of clay turns
heads and gets the attention of those around us. When that
bottle is opened, and the perfume is loosed on the breeze of
the Holy Spirit—what a fragrance!

However, if the bottle is never opened, how can the
perfume be enjoyed? What is so hard to understand is why
the bottle is so often closed tightly and set on a shelf to be
admired for what it contains. There it may sit for days, weeks,
and years, full of value but giving none. A bottle is not of
much value all by itself; it is what's inside that gives it value. It
doesn't take much effort to open the bottle so the aroma can
draw others to its source.

Jesus is the source of this wonderful bouquet, this gift of
amazing grace to all mankind. We are just channels for this
awesome, sweet scent as it flows to those within our circle of
influence. You may well be the only Christian that is able to
get the attention of someone in great need of our Savior's
sweet gift of grace.

Open the bottle and throw away the top. You can always
get a refill, but you may not be able to bring back that lost
opportunity to be the fragrance of His grace in a stinking
world.

4
Blessed Unity
✝

"That they all may be one, as You, Father, are in
Me, and I in You; that they also may be one in
Us, that the world may believe
that You sent Me."
(John 17:21)

Our potential is not altogether determined by
who we are or what our abilities are, but also by
the people with whom we join ourselves and
become one.

Be One!

"That they all may be one, as You, Father, are in Me, and I
in You; that they also may be one in Us, that the world
may believe that You sent Me." (John 17:21)

How can I be one with my brother? I can think of my
brother above myself. I can forgive my brother. I can let him
have his way (if his way is not ungodly), even if I think his
methods are wrong and will lead to shipwreck. I must let God
take care of the shipwrecks. He is the Captain of this ship,
and He knows how to direct His crew.

You say, "He hurt my feelings; I want to stay mad at him
for a while!" Is God still mad at you for the times you hurt
Him?   You think, "I can do that job better than he can." Do
you really think so? How many hours and days and nights
have you prayed and struggled over that task?

This is what the Captain says: "I pick My crew, and they
serve where I put them; judging how well they do is not your
place. I have a plan much bigger than yours; it takes all my
crew's strengths and weaknesses, and I have put them in the
place where they fit. My plan may not make sense to you, but
I know what to do to perfect it. I am building a church with
some who are strong and some who are weak, but when they
are *one*, the whole is much stronger than each individual part
alone."

Everyone is needed; all have a place on this ship of the
church. Lock arms with your neighbor, weld your heart to
his, and together obey the Captain's commands, for in the
storms that will come, it is not whether one is strong or weak,
right or wrong that will enable him to stand. The strong one
who tries to stand alone will be washed into the sea. He who
has his own sure plan that he thinks is right will not stand
without his brother. Even the one who may be wrong in his

methods will stand when he holds to the Master of the waves and does not lose his grip on his brother.

Do you want to be like the brother who thought he could weather the storm in his own strength, and was washed overboard? Are you perhaps like the brother who thought his own plan was right, who had all his ducks in a row, but drowned with them? Or, would you like to be that brother who, even though weak, held to the Captain and to his brothers?

More than our methods, weaknesses, and mistakes, it is pride that rips up *oneness*.

But love covers all sins. (Prov. 10:12)

Beloved Brother

We were all once estranged from the family of God. In the book of Philemon, we find Onesimus, a run-away slave who had come into contact with Paul and accepted Jesus as his Savior. However, Onesimus was estranged from his master Philemon, so Paul writes a letter to Philemon asking him to grant pardon to his slave.

As I read this epistle today, I saw each of us as being like Onesimus. We had run away from our Master and His purpose, seeking to satisfy our own desires, but Jesus apprehended and redeemed us. When Jesus redeems a sinner, He sends him to the church with this letter in his hand: "Therefore receive him as my own heart, a beloved brother, especially to Me."

We are commanded, as Paul commanded Philemon in this letter, to receive that one whom Christ has redeemed, no matter who he is, his station in life, or what he has done. If he owes you any thing, the Lord is saying, "Charge it to Me; it is his debt no longer, but Mine." We are commanded to forgive, receive, and make him a brother, a beloved brother. This epistle is Jesus' open letter to the church to receive as brothers all His children whom He has redeemed with His own blood.

Thank You, Lord, for making a place for each of us in your family, the Church. Let us be to You as Onesimus' name means—profitable.

If then you count me as a partner, receive him as you would me. But if he has wronged you or owes anything, put that on my account. I, Paul, am writing with my own hand. I will repay—not to mention to you that you owe me even your own self besides. Yes, brother, let me have joy from you in the Lord; refresh my heart in the Lord. Having confidence in your obedience, I write to you, knowing that you will do even more than I say. (Philem. 1:17-21)

Harmony

Harmony in the spiritual family of God (the church) and harmony in a natural family are tied together; what relates to one relates to the other. We need to study what it was that got the Israelites out of harmony with God. Then I believe we might get some insight about harmony in the family and home. Also, if we look at what brings harmony in the home, I think we can get some insight about what brings us into harmony with God. We must always look at the family as the basic unit of the church.

God wanted the Israelites to wipe out all the Cannanites so His people would not be influenced to adopt their evil ways. When Israel began to look at the ways of the heathen, they began to be drawn away from God. Today the enemy would have families adopt the ways of the heathen by making evil look good to God's people. The world's idea of the family is distorted, yet we let it pour into our living rooms everyday.

It seemed a very hard thing when God said go in and kill all the Cannanites—men, women, and children—leave none alive (not even the animals, in some cases). It also seems a hard thing to cast away all things that would cause us to look with longing on the world's life style. We reason with ourselves, "It can be used for such good." Saul said the same thing when Samuel asked him why he heard bleating of sheep, when God said destroy them all. Saul said, "I planned to offer a great sacrifice to God."

Several times in my life God has led me to totally do away with something until I could learn to use it for only good purposes. God did not tell Israel to destroy all the animals of the enemy every time, but sometimes it was necessary, so that they would learn to value God's Word more than the possessions of this world. When this lesson is learned, then the possessions can be used the right way.

Potential

What can a man and a woman accomplish in their marriage? Is there a limit to what they can become? Is each limited or made better by the other? I believe each of these questions can have a positive or a negative answer, leaving each couple to choose which they will accept. Every couple has the potential to rise as high as the strengths, or sink as low as the weaknesses of each spouse. Which will you choose? God's plan is for strong marriages; the devil's plan is to destroy marriages. If we choose God's way, He will magnify each of our strengths as we allow Him.

This works the same way in the church, the bride of Christ. It is His desire for us to be like Him in every way. Again, it is our choice. We can join ourselves to Him and let Him form us into His image. *Oh, to be like Him!*

You may often look at your husband or wife and think, "I can't do what he can do," or "I can never have that strength that I see in her." God has made you one with that husband or that wife, and as you walk in unity, you can let each other's strengths and abilities become your own. So, in the same way, we must let Christ's strengths and abilities become ours while we walk as one with Him in every area of our lives. Just as our spouses complement and complete us, so Christ gives strength to our weaknesses and makes our strong points stronger.

Our potential is not altogether determined by who we are or what our abilities are, but also by the people with whom we join ourselves and become one. The mightiest soldier in the world can join himself to a weak and poorly-led army that will lose the war; a weak and puny boy can join a great and mighty army with a great general that wins all the victories. Which of the two do you think will march in the victory parade?

5
Grow in Faith
✝

Now faith is the substance of things hoped for, the evidence of things not seen. For by it the elders obtained a good testimony.
(Hebrews 11:1-2)

Faith is not a dream world; faith is reality in the hands of God. Faith produces a life of action; we do not always know where it will lead, but we always know He is leading.

Faith's Connection

But without faith it is impossible to please Him, for he who comes to God must believe that He is, and that He is a rewarder of those who diligently seek Him. (Heb 11:6)

Our faith is rooted in our relationship with God. If we know Him, love Him, and desire to please Him, then we act accordingly; we keep His commandments. We sin when we rebel and do whatever is contrary to His Word.

It may be argued that we can delude ourselves into believing what pleases us is right, even if it is wrong according to scripture. I would agree we can delude ourselves, but if we seek God with a whole heart daily and study His Word, we will grow in our walk with the Master. Then we will not go very long without understanding when something we are doing is breaking our fellowship with Him.

If we are aware that a particular thing in our lives is breaking our fellowship with the Lord, but we can find nothing in the Bible about the subject, then is the time to check our attitude about what we are doing. It may be that a wrong attitude needs to be corrected. If that does not settle the matter, then lay it before the Lord and be willing to sacrifice it to Him. Our willingness may be all that is required, because even good things can become little gods to us, and nothing must come between us and God. Be willing to give it up and walk away from it. Some things may not be a problem for others, but may get between you and God.

I have on several occasions laid something down for a time. I also found I had to leave other things behind forever. I do not look back with longing for those things, because I am so happy in my Lord. Children, you can lay nothing down that God will not replace with much more than what you discarded. I have lived it and know it is true.

Faith's Treasure

> In this you greatly rejoice, though now for a little while, if
> need be, you have been grieved by various trials, that the
> genuineness of your faith, being much more precious than
> gold that perishes, though it is tested by fire, may be found
> to praise, honor, and glory at the revelation of Jesus Christ.
> (1Peter 1:6-7)

This family has so much in which to rejoice. God in His
mercy has given us such a great spiritual inheritance! Yet, for
a little while in this life we are distressed. Today I have been
feeling greatly distressed by my job. I wanted so badly to just
walk away, but I didn't. There have been many times that my
faith has been tried through all sorts of problems that seemed
to be impossible to overcome. Through the power of God, I
did triumph and found that with each victory my faith grew a
little stronger than before.

Faith grows through struggles. Many of our brothers in
Christ face intense distress daily. In some parts of the world,
mobs want to exterminate Christians. In other countries,
churches are outlawed and many Christians are imprisoned.
His grace is sufficient for them; His grace is sufficient for me;
His grace is sufficient for you.

It is only a little while, my children, and trials will all be
past. God knows how to prove our faith, which is so very
precious to Him, more precious than we can imagine. Let
your faith grow and abound! Let it leap to heaven! Let it
bound over the piddling little trials of this life!

What is the treasure that we lay up in Heaven? It is made
up largely of the victories of our faith, which are the building
blocks to everything good we could ever do and ever hope to
hold as an eternal treasure. Let us choose to allow faith to
grow and abound that it "may be found to result in praise and
glory and honor at the revelation of Jesus Christ."

Faith's Seed

Blessed be the God and Father of our Lord Jesus Christ,
who according to His abundant mercy has begotten us
again to a living hope through the resurrection of Jesus
Christ from the dead, to an inheritance incorruptible and
undefiled and that does not fade away, reserved in heaven
for you, who are kept by the power of God through faith
for salvation ready to be revealed in the last time. (1 Peter
1:3-5)

Jesus made a way for us to come before the very throne
of God! Oh, what an inheritance He has given! It cannot be
destroyed! It will not change! This inheritance has been
reserved especially for you!

All of God's power is at your disposal to protect this
salvation. He also has put something in your hand. It is a *seed
of faith* (see Matt. 17:20 and Rom. 12:3) that you are to hold
up like a shield. You may think, "What kind of shield would a
tiny little seed be in battle?" Well, I'll ask, "What good is a
scepter in the hand of a ruler?" It is the symbol of great
authority. That seed of faith in your *open hand* is a symbol of
the power of God.

I have often heard it said that you must hold on to your
faith, as if by your own strength, but I believe it is more
accurate to say faith is held in your open hand that is
extended upward to God. We do not have to grasp tightly
with our feeble grip—God is the power that holds, moves,
and controls all things. Trust and abide in God's love and live
in fellowship with Him; then, faith will grow and abound
naturally in your life.

What is this seed of faith that grows in our lives? The
words we speak produce faith, or more accurately, the
thoughts that we accept as fact, whether we speak the words
or not. When we truly believe, we will speak words that cause

faith to grow; conversely, when we lack faith we will speak words that cause unbelief to grow.

Let me illustrate how our words can affect our fellowship with God. I was experiencing confidence and faith in God, along with a wonderful peace, as I was walking with my Jesus. Then, all of a sudden, everything went all wrong; my peace flew away, and I was filled with uneasiness. Someone had said something to me that seemed very logical and sensible, and I had voiced my agreement with the statement. That is the point at which my peace left, but I did not realize it until the next day during my morning prayer, when I heard this in my spirit: *"Those words expressed doubt in My provision for you."* I knew then from where my uneasiness came; it came from words out of my own mouth.

Put your trust in God, think thoughts of faith, and speak words of faith. God will take care of you, bless you, and lead you. Our faith is very important to God. It is tied directly to our love for Him, our peace, and our fellowship with Him. Faith is not a tool God has given us to claim and grab hold of what we want. It is a settled trust that God knows what is best for us, loves us with an everlasting love, and hears our prayers.

God will empower the seed of faith you allow Him to plant in your life—words of trust, confidence, and surety of His love for you.

Your faith is the title deed to the kingdom, and it pleases God more than anything you could ever accomplish in all your life.

> Above all, taking the shield of faith with which you will be able to quench all the fiery darts of the wicked one. (Eph. 6:16)

> "If you have faith as a mustard seed, you will say to this mountain, 'Move from here to there,' and it will move; and nothing will be impossible for you." (Matt. 17:20)

Faith's Conviction

So whatever you believe about these things keep between yourself and God. Blessed is the man who does not condemn himself by what he approves. But the man who has doubts is condemned if he eats, because his eating is not from faith; and everything that does not come from faith is sin. (Rom. 14:22-23 NIV)

It is good that you have convictions by which you live. However, what if your convictions are not just like those of your fellow Christian? Are you trying to please your brother, or God? Is your brother trying to please you, or God? Though we all have our own set of convictions, most of them should be the same as those of our Christian brothers, because we have the same Word as a guide book. If you have a few convictions that are unique to you, they are to be just between you and God; do not in any way use them to hurt your brother.

If you feel condemned by what you believe, you need to take a hard look at what you believe, because something is wrong that needs to be corrected. If there is a doubt about what you are doing, then your conviction is not coming from faith. Then from where does that doubtful conviction come? Maybe it comes from convenience, pride, lust, or just plain laziness. Whatever the source, the doubtful conviction does not come from faith, and if it does not come from faith, then it is sin, pure and simple.

You say, "But I only do what I see other Christians do." Maybe it is sin for everyone, or maybe just for you. What you do must come from your faith, not your brother's faith. What do you really believe?

Our convictions may change slightly as we grow in the Lord, but they must always be grounded in the Word and faith.

The enemy of our souls likes to try to change what we believe; he does it very subtly. Satan would like to change your compass that points you to God by adjusting it off true north just one degree a day; before long, you are going in the opposite direction and do not even realize the change.

We all find ourselves in our own unique set of circumstances that affect our thinking about how we should live as Christians. Though some of our ideas may be shaped by our culture, and some may be developed by our experiences, *truth is not relative; it is concrete.* When we study the Word and pray, we will see what our Lord has to say about each situation. God does not, however, put all of us in the same mold. Each of us is unique, and God will treat us as such. Hence, there may be some very small number of convictions that are yours alone.

> Therefore, my beloved, as you have always obeyed, not as in my presence only, but now much more in my absence, work out your own salvation with fear and trembling; for it is God who works in you both to will and to do for His good pleasure. (Phil. 2:12-13)

Faith's Assurance

> Now faith is the substance of things hoped for, the
> evidence of things not seen. For by it the elders obtained a
> good testimony. By faith we understand that the worlds
> were framed by the word of God, so that the things which
> are seen were not made of things which are visible. (Heb.
> 11:1-3)

In this scripture we find a definition of faith. The two key
words are *substance* and *evidence*. Substance is the reality that
removes doubt, so we might say that faith is like soap for the
soul; it washes out the spots of doubt and cleanses us from
the grime of unbelief. Faith is the opposite of doubt, so the
more faith we have, the less doubt we have. The reverse is
also true. God gave us hope where there was none, and faith
washes the windows of the mind so we can clearly see that
for which we hope. Evidence persuades us of the truth; we
are sure, even though the eyes cannot see. We know Him and
know He is true.

We also see throughout the eleventh chapter of Hebrews
that holy men of God did great things, though it was not the
great things they did which gained them God's approval; it
was their faith. They did not doubt Him, but were totally
persuaded that God's Word could not fail. Faith was a way of
life, a mode of thought, and the lens through which these
men and women saw all things.

By faith they were able to understand that God created
from the invisible the things that are visible. Science only
understands what it can measure. Faith does not measure; it
just believes. These folks in the Bible failed at times, just as
we do, but their life perspective was one of faith; they never
stopped believing God. Keep the faith, guys; if you do
nothing else, keep the faith.

True Thoughts

> Finally, brethren, whatever things are true, whatever things
> are noble, whatever things are just, whatever things are
> pure, whatever things are lovely, whatever things are of
> good report, if there is any virtue and if there is anything
> praiseworthy—meditate on these things. (Phil. 4:8)

What have you been thinking about today? Were your
thoughts true, noble, just, pure, lovely, and of good report?
Who we really are is exposed in our thought life.

First, let's look at the word *true* and all it implies. To be
true is to be genuine. Too often, we let impostors get into our
minds masquerading as genuine. Lust tries to pass itself off as
love. Prideful thoughts masquerade as honesty. Covetousness
claims to be faith. These little disguised thieves are sometimes
too hard for us to expose; it takes the Holy Spirit to rip off
their masks. The Bible is pure truth and will expose anything
and everything that is false as we read it in the light of the
Holy Spirit. From time to time, we may even lie to ourselves
and tell ourselves what we want to hear because it pleases the
flesh. Don't neglect the reading of the Word; saturate your
mind with God's Word; then, truth will prevail in your
thought life and lies will be exposed.

To be true is to be real. Do I think in terms of truth and
reality, or does my mind dwell only on fantasy? I have always
been a daydreamer, so I can understand how someone can
live in a fantasy world mentally. I can sit for hours making up
stories in my mind, or replaying and expanding stories I saw
on TV. Therefore, I have been compelled by this verse to
repent and to focus my mind on what is true and real. I do
not believe it is wrong to dream, but dreams must be kept in
control. Think on what is true, and don't let fantasy drown
out reality.

Faith's Reality

At times I slip into a dream world of what I would want to be, to do, and to have. However, as I live for a while in my perfect dream world, I realize it does not accomplish anything useful, and gets me nowhere. I must come back to reality to go forward in my life. Reality, so often, can be depressing; that is why I slip into the dream world in the first place. If reality is depressing and the dream world is useless, what am I to do?

Live in faith's reality! Faith is not a dream world and it is not depressing; faith is reality in the hands of God. He takes what is good of the dreams, and in the reality of His power builds in us a vision of what can be and what will be, as we walk step by step in the light He gives us daily.

A dreamboat is a big ship that has run aground and is going nowhere. It is impossible to guide a ship that is stuck in the mud and has no motion. A little rowboat, on the other hand, is not as elegant or as big, but if it is being rowed along, it can be guided because it is in motion. Faith's reality is in the little rowboat; we row and trust God's hand on the rudder to guide us to the port He chooses.

Don't run your ship of life aground and dream of distant ports that you will never reach. Keep on rowing in faith's reality, and as you go along, you will see more clearly where you are going and what you need to do when you get there.

It is good to wait on the Lord, but many times He is saying move on into the unknown. Yet we keep waiting because we cannot see what the other shore holds for us. We go nowhere and do nothing and call it faith, when what we really have is quite the opposite of faith.

Faith is not a dream world; faith is reality in the hands of God. Faith produces a life of action; we do not always know where it will lead, but we always know He is leading.

Faith's Grasp

> In this you greatly rejoice, though now for a little while, if
> need be, you have been grieved by various trials, that the
> genuineness of your faith, being much more precious than
> gold that perishes, though it is tested by fire, may be found
> to praise, honor, and glory at the revelation of Jesus Christ,
> whom having not seen you love. Though now you do not
> see Him, yet believing, you rejoice with joy inexpressible
> and full of glory, receiving the end of your faith—the
> salvation of your souls. (1 Peter 1:6-9)

Throughout our lives, while we are guarding and growing
that faith that we were given, we can greatly rejoice in this: we
have a "salvation ready to be revealed in the last time" (1
Peter 1:5). We are fully saved if we have made Jesus the Lord
of our lives, but we must hold to faith to see the ultimate end
of that salvation. Faith is that unbreakable cord by which we
were saved and drawn out of the pit of sin. That same cord of
faith will keep us through all life's troubles and carry us into
the eternal presence of God Himself. Don't let doubt or fear
cause you to loosen your grip. Don't let abundance of earthly
things entice you to grasp another cord. Through the fire and
through the flood, keep holding to the cord of faith.

I picture in my mind a very deep pit with an unending
cord coiled at the bottom, which is continually being drawn
out of the pit by the hand of Jesus, toward the eternal light of
God above. In the pit are many people; some rich, some
poor, some strong, some weak. These people can choose to
grasp the cord, look up, and spend their earthly life joyfully,
being drawn to the light, or they can choose to doubt the
strength of the one holding the cord, and continue their
earthly existence wandering in the dark depths of the pit.
Some shout encouragement to others to grab the cord and
hold tight. Others grow fearful that the Strong One at the top
will not be able to hold them; they persuade many to follow
them as they release their grip and fall back into the dark pit.

Our God is not gathering from the pit a group of people based on whether they are rich, poor, brilliant, great humanitarians, or foolish, but whether they have been purified by faith in Him as they make the trip up to His light. As a pleased Father, He takes the faithful in His arms, hugs them, and gives them great rewards. They have praised, glorified, and honored Him by simply holding on with a tenacious grip to that faith that He put in their hands.

But to him who does not work but believes on Him who justifies the ungodly, his faith is accounted for righteousness. (Rom 4:5)

Faith is the simplest of all things, and perhaps because of its simplicity it is more difficult to explain. What is faith? It is made up of three things—knowledge, belief, and trust. "How shall they believe in him whom they have not heard?"...

Better the poorest real faith actually at work, than the best ideal of it left in the region of speculation. The great matter is to believe on the Lord Jesus at once. Never mind distinctions and definitions. A hungry man eats though he does not understand the composition of his food, the anatomy of his mouth, or the process of digestion: he lives because he eats. Another far more clever person understands thoroughly the science of nutrition; but if he does not eat he will die, with all his knowledge. There are, no doubt, many at this hour in Hell who understand the doctrine of faith, but did not believe. On the other hand, not one who has trusted in the Lord Jesus has ever been cast out, though he may never have been able intelligently to define his faith.

(From *All of Grace*, PD, by Charles H. Spurgeon)

Atmosphere of Faith

Jesus did not perform many healings or miracles where unbelief was apparent in people around Him, but where there was an atmosphere of faith, supernatural power always poured forth from the Master. If we are looking for the miraculous power of God, then shouldn't we be looking for faith?

How do we gain faith? "So then faith comes by hearing, and hearing by the Word of God" (Rom. 10:17). Where does the Word of God direct us? It directs us to Jesus. We are not looking for miracles or for faith, but for Jesus. Faith is not something we can generate within ourselves to see God work. "Now faith is being sure of what we hope for and certain of what we do not see" (Heb. 11:1 NIV). How can we be sure of what we hope for and certain of what we do not see? Because we know Jesus, He places that surety in our hearts. We are confident in Him no matter what happens because we know who He is and where we stand with Him.

Job knew God in that way when he said, "Though he slay me, yet will I trust in him" (Job 13:15 KJV). Because Paul and Silas had this confidence, they were able to sing praises to God while bound in stocks in the Philippian jail. Daniel had faith in his Master, even when he spent the night in the lion's den. Shadrach, Meshach, and Abednego knew who would walk with them through the fire. Many others have also known the Lord in the same way as they drew their last breath on earth before being lifted into His waiting arms.

The atmosphere of faith that gives birth to the mighty works of God in His church is born of an intimate fellowship between the church and her King, Jesus. Let us know Him and live in the atmosphere of faith.

Yet indeed I also count all things loss for the excellence of the knowledge of Christ Jesus my Lord, for whom I have suffered the loss of all things, and count them as rubbish, that I may gain Christ and be found in Him, not having my own righteousness, which is from the law, but that which is through faith in Christ, the righteousness which is from God by faith; that I may know Him and the power of His resurrection, and the fellowship of His sufferings, being conformed to His death, if, by any means, I may attain to the resurrection from the dead. Not that I have already attained, or am already perfected; but I press on, that I may lay hold of that for which Christ Jesus has also laid hold of me. (Phil. 3:8-12)

The View

Where do you choose to settle?
Will you make your nest in the swamp of worry and fear?
Or will you build your cabin on the peak of challenge
And enjoy the view?

You decide whether you want to hide
Or put forth the effort to climb the mountainside.
You can't change the weather or the circumstances,
But you can change the view.
So what will you do?
It is up to you!

Will you view your life through the eyes of reason?
Or will you view your life through faith this season?
Faith is a much better view,
And it's the best life for you.

All Things Are Yours

Therefore let no one boast in men. For all things are yours:
(1 Cor. 3:21)
And you are Christ's, and Christ is God's. (1 Cor. 3:23)

What are the "all things" spoken of in this portion of
scripture? They are all you need, with no limitations, no fine
print, and no exceptions—everything you will ever need to
fulfill your purpose. "What is my purpose for being here on
Earth?" you may ask. It is for His purpose that you are here
in this time and in this place, and He will spare nothing to
fulfill that purpose if you choose to live your life for Him.

If you have accepted the gospel, you are part of the family
of God and you are heir of all things your Father owns. Life
or death of the flesh makes no difference; the gospel has
carried you into the Spirit Kingdom of God.

All things are yours "and you are Christ's and Christ is
God's." When we look at life in this way, we see things in a
new perspective, God's perspective, and the things we
thought were so important are not so important anymore. If
we know all things are ours, then there is no need to claim
anything or grasp and hold tight to anything; we already have
title to all things if we are in Christ.

We receive title to all things by faith. Stop depending on
your senses and depend on God. All things are yours, but you
cannot claim or possess them by force of will, or hard work,
or even by much prayer. All things are yours by faith in the
Maker of all things.

6
Good Thoughts
✝

Let the words of my mouth, and the meditation
of my heart, be acceptable in thy sight, O LORD,
my strength, and my redeemer.
(Psalms 19:14 KJV)

The mind is the greenhouse for what will
ultimately be planted in the garden of my life.
Destroy the diseased seedlings in the mind
before they bring death to the soul.

Noble Thoughts

Whatever things are noble, ... meditate on these things.
(Phil. 4:8)

Today I want to talk about *noble* thinking. Let us first look
at noble thoughts as they relate to other people. Can you
picture Jesus smiling at someone, and at the same time,
thinking hateful thoughts about that person? I cannot. I can,
however, see myself thinking bad thoughts about someone
whom I find irritating, or about someone who is grouchy or
angry at work; too often, I find my thoughts about these
people are the opposite of noble. Jesus spoke these words
from the cross: "Father, forgive them; for they know not
what they do" (Luke 23:34 KJV). All that I know of Jesus
tells me that in His mind were thoughts of love and
forgiveness for the men that were putting Him to death. Yet,
we sometimes think malicious thoughts about those who only
aggravate us. *Lord, help me to be noble and think noble thoughts.*

In this sinful world we live in everyday, there is much that
draws us away from what is noble or honorable, but there are
some things we can do to keep our minds on the right track.
Control what is put into your mind; don't just
indiscriminately soak up everything around you; choose good,
noble, righteous words and thoughts, even though you may
have to search a little harder to find them. You control what
you read; you control the TV; you choose when to walk away.

Turn your eyes to the Lord and His Word. Walk with the
Holy Spirit. Let Him share His thoughts with you, and don't
dwell on any thought you would not want to share with Him.

What you allow to flood into your mind will have an
impact on your thoughts, so make it a little easier to think
those good noble thoughts by keeping your mental antivirus
program turned on to block out the worthless.

Righteous Thoughts

Whatever things are just, ... meditate on these things.
(Phil. 4:8)

Thinking justly is the topic today. *Just*, or *right* as it is also
translated, is a word used to describe people who do their
duty toward God and men. Maybe our thoughts are not
always brilliant, but are they righteous? Even if we come to
the wrong conclusion, did we come to it for the right
reasons? It doesn't take a genius to think justly; even the
simplest mind can think right thoughts.

Thoughts that put God in His true place of honor, and
man in his place as a being made in the image of God, are
right thoughts. What are some examples of thoughts that fit
this description? A mind that is worshipping and loving God
is thinking justly and rightly. Our thoughts about other
people should come from an attitude of love and a desire to
see good come to all men. Too often, we are not even
thinking about God at all, and if we think about people, our
thoughts are not good. Every day of my life, I could use some
improvements in my thinking about people; at times, I have
thought to myself that I don't even like people.

The ways of Jesus are just. He loves people, even me. I
believe as Jesus walked upon the earth with a heart of love,
He was continually thinking about how to bring people to the
Father. *Lord, let my thoughts always lift You up and seek to draw men
to You!*

"Blessed are they which do hunger and thirst after
righteousness: for they shall be filled." (Matt. 5:6 KJV)

Pure Thoughts

Whatever things are pure,... meditate on these things.
(Phil. 4:8)

What are pure things? In the Greek language, this word *pure* comes, from the same root word as the word *holy*. The Word of God is pure; think on it. Another way to describe pure is clean and undefiled. Doesn't it sound as if I am describing the mind of Christ? Isn't the mind of Christ what we desire to have? Jesus is our role model. His purity that overcame all sin was first a purity of mind. The mind dwells on evil before the body commits evil; if the mind is clean, the life is clean. We may not be able to keep an evil thought from passing by, but we can refuse to stand in the middle of the road and get run over by it.

Far too many people pattern their thinking after the culture in which they live and then mix it with Christianity to get just what suits them. It may look good and sound good, but is it pure?

The mind is like a garden. It needs to be fertilized with the Word and watered by communion with the One who is holy. We have to pull out the weeds (wicked thoughts); otherwise, they will overtake and choke out the pure crop (good thoughts). We need to put up a good strong fence around the garden and know when to close the eye and ear gates, because if the ravenous beasts get past the eyes and ears, they will devour the harvest with envy, lust, and pride.

"Blessed are the pure in heart: for they shall see God."
(Matt. 5:8 KJV)

Lovely Thoughts

> Whatever things are lovely,... meditate on these things.
> (Phil. 4:8)

What does *lovely* mean in this verse? *Pleasing* and *agreeable* appear to be the best synonyms. If thoughts are pleasing and agreeable, they are bridging the gap between two opposing forces, bringing them toward love and away from division. Are my thoughts bringing God, others, and me together in love? If division is what my thoughts are brewing up, I have lost my way. A heart of love is so much better, both for me and for the other person!

Some people seem to enjoy holding on to a grudge, and nothing will pry it from their minds. I have many faults, but I thank God that holding on to anger has always made me physically ill; I would rather apologize, even if I'm right, and forgive and forget as soon as possible. (I don't like being ill.)

What kind of attitude and demeanor do you have in your daily life? Would people call your disposition lovely, or would they say that you are an old grouch? What is in our thoughts will be revealed in our words and in our actions. Peace must be made first in our own thoughts before it can be made between ourselves and others. Think lovely thoughts and let those lead to lovely relationships.

> "Blessed are the peacemakers: for they shall be called the children of God." (Matt. 5:9 KJV)

Respectful Thoughts

Whatever things are of good report,... meditate on these
things. (Phil. 4:8)

A *good report* will bless and not destroy a good reputation.
We tend to put individuals or groups of people in classes, for
example: good or bad; smart or ignorant; rich or poor; this
race or that race; people I like or people I don't like. We don't
like the rich man because we think he is a snob, or we don't
like the poor man because we think he is lazy. We don't like
either the loud-mouthed person or the quiet one. We think
lawyers and doctors charge too much, or we think all carnival
workers and salesmen are crooks. I could go on and on, but I
think you get the picture. If we dig deep enough, we all will
find some group or class of people we do not want to give a
good report of in our thoughts.

Our thoughts bring a good report or bad report out of
our mouths. It has been said, "If you can't say anything good
about a person, don't say anything at all." I'm not saying look
only for the good and ignore the bad in people, but look for
the potential for God to bring about change in them. If we
meditate on what we dislike about people, our wrong
attitudes become worse than what we perceived in them. It
may be that what we dislike about people actually originates
in our own bad attitudes. *Lord, help me to be as merciful to people
in my thoughts as I would want them to be to me!*

"Blessed are the merciful: for they shall obtain mercy."
(Matt. 5:7 KJV).

Virtuous Thoughts

If there is any virtue and if there is anything
praiseworthy—meditate on these things. (Phil. 4:8)

Virtue includes moral excellence and goodness. Our
meditations should be the very best of what is true, noble,
just, pure, lovely, and of good report. The goal here is not just
to think about what will be acceptable, but what would be the
best. If we only aim to get it right the majority of the time, we
are not aiming for excellence, but for mediocrity.

Jesus was and is the most virtuous man that ever lived;
He is our pattern to follow. If we are to be an example of
virtue to whomever we influence, we must be like Him.
Virtue is not something tangible you can put into someone's
hand; it comes from deep within the heart. How does that
virtue develop deep in the heart? We plant it there by what
we allow to enter the mind, grow, and mature there.

Things that are *praiseworthy* turn our thoughts to an
attitude of praise to God. If the body is the temple of the
Spirit, then the mind is the Holy of Holies. Nothing unclean
could go into the Holy of Holies; only what was perfectly
pleasing to God could enter. Do my thoughts please God, or
do they only please me? The mind is the greenhouse for what
will ultimately be planted in the garden of my life. Destroy the
diseased seedlings in the mind before they bring death to the
soul.

"Ye are the salt of the earth." (Matt. 5:13 KJV)

7
Practice Godliness
✝

Whatever you have learned or received
or heard from me, or seen in me—
put it into practice.
(Philippians 4:9 NIV)

A godly life does not happen by accident;
You have got to learn it and live it.
If you are willing to practice,
The Holy Spirit is ready to work through you.

Respect the Workers

> And we urge you, brethren, to recognize those who labor
> among you, and are over you in the Lord and admonish
> you, and to esteem them very highly in love for their
> work's sake. Be at peace among yourselves. (1 Thess. 5:12-
> 13)

These verses surely apply to pastors and elders in the
church, and to any person actively laboring in the kingdom of
God. The word that is translated here as *recognize* is also
translated as know, appreciate, or respect. It is clear that that
this scripture tells us to respect all of our fellow laborers in
Christ.

Let me illustrate this passage with a little story: A janitor
is mopping the hall in a big company office. The company
president walks by, not even noticing the janitor and the
janitor thinks to himself, "Just another snob in a three-piece
suit." Let's change this story and see the difference: A janitor
is mopping the hall and the company president walks by and
says, "Good morning, John. You are doing a good job." The
janitor says, "Good morning, Sir. I'm glad to see the company
stock going up." To know, appreciate, and respect your
fellow laborer is good in the work place, but essential in the
church.

Now, let's look at that word *admonish*. To admonish is to
give instruction. Pastors and teachers are very important
sources of instruction, but never forget that you can learn
something from everybody. This scripture does not say,
"Esteem very highly in love those that do things your way."
Instead, we are urged to "esteem very highly in love the
laborers for their work's sake." Love and respect all those
working for the kingdom of Christ; honor the elders; be at
peace among yourselves. These two verses, if taken to heart,
will stop much division in the church.

Encourage the Brethren

> Now we exhort you, brethren, warn those who are unruly, comfort the fainthearted, uphold the weak, be patient with all. See that no one renders evil for evil to anyone, but always pursue what is good both for yourselves and for all. (1 Thess. 5:14-15)

Paul writes here by the Holy Spirit, telling the brethren how to treat one another. To exhort means to urge. This is not just a recommendation; it is important instruction to the church.

We don't want to get involved with the unruly or the weak brethren. When it comes to the unruly, too often we are afraid to warn them. "Let someone else do it," we say. It takes prayer, it takes time, and it takes patience, but it is worth it to commit yourself to the task of helping your brother. Those who get involved may get a little dirty, but they also may save a brother. *Thank You, Lord, for taking time to help me. Thank You for the people who patiently encouraged me.*

We say, "I have too many troubles of my own; I don't have time to nurse the weak and fainthearted." Remember that the Lord is always patient with us, and never gives up! He is patient with everybody! You will find that if you reach out to others and pour yourself into their lives much more will be poured into your own life. Be a channel of blessing, not a stagnant pool of fear and selfishness.

We claim we have a right to repay those who mistreat us, but God has reserved that right for Himself only; it never was, nor ever can be ours. We are instructed to "always pursue what is good" for everybody, not just for ourselves. He who pursues does not walk casually along, but runs with all his might to reach the goal.

Rejoice

Rejoice always. (1 Thess. 5:16)

It is hard to understand how someone could *rejoice always*. Sometimes I don't feel like rejoicing; sometimes I'm too busy with life's problems to even think about rejoicing.

How is it possible to rejoice always? How could Paul, of all people, with all the trials he went through, rejoice always? If you remember, it was at Philippi that Paul and Silas continued to rejoice in the Savior, even after they had been beaten and put in stocks in the inner prison. Paul visited Thessalonica soon after he left Philippi. He founded churches in these two cities and later wrote epistles to the Philippians and Thessalonians. What was it that Paul had learned about rejoicing even before his experience in the Philippian jail? I believe Paul understood the love of his Savior, and nothing else mattered to him but that love. This is part of what he wrote to the church at Philippi:

> But what things were gain to me, these I have counted loss for Christ. Yet indeed I also count all things loss for the excellence of the knowledge of Christ Jesus my Lord, for whom I have suffered the loss of all things, and count them as rubbish, that I may gain Christ and be found in Him, not having my own righteousness, which is from the law, but that which is through faith in Christ, the righteousness which is from God by faith. (Phil. 3:7-9)

Paul was not rejoicing in blessings or the good things he had received, but he was rejoicing in the fact that Jesus loved him enough to save him. That was enough for Paul. If we can see the depths of our Savior's love as Paul saw it, then we can rejoice always, just as he did.

Pray Always

Pray without ceasing. (1 Thess. 5:17)

Why should we pray without ceasing? How can we pray without ceasing?

I look at my life and realize that everything good in my life could be taken away so easily. It seems, and I suppose it is so, that each of our lives is held by only a thread. The enemy of our souls likes to show us every knife that could cut that thread of life. It can be good from time to time for us to see how frail we are and how inadequate our efforts are, but we cannot live in a state of fear; we only need pass through fear long enough to again be reminded that the thread holding us is the mighty power of God, and nothing outside of ourselves can cut it. Prayer is our lifeline to the power of God; that is why we pray.

There are times when we are compelled to pray and intercede for some great need. This prayer is fixed in our minds until we are assured that our Good Master will bring the answer by and by; then we move on. There is also the time we set aside each day to get alone with God, but this, too, comes to an end. Then, there is that fellowship we have with Jesus as we go through the day, but even that must be interrupted by our work.

Think of this unceasing prayer as a car motor that is always running. Our verbal and mental prayers are like the different gears of the transmission which tap into that motor's vast power. If that motor stops running, we can shift gears all day, but we will go nowhere.

Prayer is the soul's breath of life. You can stop breathing, but not for long, or you will die. Keep praying, even when you don't feel like it. You may not always have a sense of God's presence when you pray, but He is always there.

Give Thanks

In everything give thanks; for this is the will of God in
Christ Jesus for you. (1 Thess. 5:18)

It has always been my desire to be thankful. Even if I
receive no other blessing in this life, I feel that I have been
blessed beyond measure. However, this scripture does not say
give thanks because you are blessed; it doesn't even mention
blessing. We are not told to give thanks *for* everything, but *in*
everything. Wherever we are, in whatever circumstance, we
are to give thanks to God; in so doing, we are obeying God's
will. If we live in a fine mansion—if we are prisoners in a
dungeon—if we are well fed—if we are hungry—we give
thanks. Because we want to please God, and because we love
Him, we give thanks.

There is nothing greater for which to give thanks than for
His mercy. I find ten verses in the Bible where these words
are found together: "give thanks"..."for his mercy endureth
for ever" (KJV). It pleases the heart of our Lord when we are
thankful for the blood He shed for us. You may sometimes
feel you have nothing for which to be thankful; just
remember His mercy and give thanks. You may be in great
distress; just remember His mercy and give thanks.
Remember always to rejoice in His love and give thanks for
His mercy, which truly does endure forever. Ten thousand
years from now we may seldom think of our time on earth,
but every minute we will be rejoicing in His love and giving
thanks for His mercy.

Keep Listening

Do not quench the Spirit. Do not despise prophecies. (1 Thess. 5:19-20)

Don't put out the fire of the Spirit. Listen to the words of prophecy. We are temples of the Holy Spirit; He dwells within us, and if we will only listen, He will speak to us day by day. Frequently, we think we have everything figured out and don't need any guidance. I can say from experience, that attitude is always wrong. More often than not, we are lost in the jungle of life and don't even realize it. We quench the Spirit when we refuse to hear what He has to say about a subject. Remember, the Spirit knows everything, so it is best if you listen.

God may speak to us through another person, though sometimes that person may be saying something we don't want to hear. Listen to the prophet of God. Prophecy most often means declaring the counsel of God. You may hear this word of counsel from your pastor's sermon, from a friend, or maybe even from a stranger. Don't discard the prophetic word because it does not fit your plans; maybe your plans need a change or a little adjustment. Listen for His voice; it comes in many ways; don't quench it or despise it.

Of course we must not believe that every word we hear is a prophecy from God. He will confirm His word to you and make it certain in your mind if you keep listening intently to Him. Peace of mind is a good indication that the Spirit is speaking to you. The Spirit's message to us may not be what we want to hear, it may not fit our plans, and it may even seem foolish. Instead of suppressing the prophecy, judge it by the Word of God and by your inner peace or lack thereof.

Keep Looking

> Test all things; hold fast what is good. Abstain from every
> form of evil. (1 Thess. 5:21-22)

We must always keep our spiritual eyes open, being
watchful in every situation. Not everything is true, and not
everything is real; there is always a counterfeit trying to pass
itself off as the real thing. The enemy of our souls would try
to disguise himself as the Spirit of God. There are more than
a few false prophets. Evil may even be advertised as good by
the spirits of hell.

I don't know all the answers, but I have learned a few
things. God is never in a hurry, and He has no emergencies.
If you hear a voice in your spirit screaming, "You must act
now; it is an emergency," it is not God. On the contrary,
when you hear the calm, peaceful voice of the Spirit of God,
listen. One day as I drove home from work in my usual rush,
I heard the gentle, calm voice of the spirit say, *"Slow down,
son."* I slowed down, not feeling stressed out at all. Within
two blocks, a little girl about 5 years old ran out in front of
me and I hit my brakes, stopping only inches from her. When
I have listened to that "hurry-up spirit," I have never seen any
good come of it, except more hurry-up emergency calls
claiming to be from God. The enemy would like to drive us
before him with a big stick, but the true Spirit of God leads
calmly, like a shepherd.

> For God is not the author of confusion but of peace. (1
> Cor. 14:33)

There are three tests that will help you determine if the
Spirit of God is speaking the words you hear. Test the spirits
and the prophets by what they say about Jesus, by whether
the world likes their message, and by the love that you see in
them.

The Jesus Test: Is Jesus lifted up?

By this you know the Spirit of God: Every spirit that
confesses that Jesus Christ has come in the flesh is of God.
(1 John 4:2)

The Who-Likes-It Test: To whom does it appeal?

They are of the world. Therefore they speak as of the
world, and the world hears them. (1 John 4:5)

The Love Test: Is there love in it?

Beloved, let us love one another, for love is of God; and
everyone who loves is born of God and knows God. (1
John 4:7)

If you find any evil in anything, leave it alone. Don't try to
see how close to the world you can get, but seek to walk as
close to God you can. You wouldn't play with a deadly snake;
don't play with sin, either. All sin is deadly; some sins take
longer to kill you than others, but all come to the same
conclusion.

How to Prosper

> And in every work that he began in the service of the
> house of God, in the law and in the commandment, to
> seek his God, he did it with all his heart. So he prospered.
> (2 Chron. 31:21)

How often do we try to figure out how to become
prosperous? Consider what it means to prosper as the Lord
would want us to prosper. Understanding this will take some
soul searching, prayer, and study of God's Word. Prosperity
comes to those, like Hezekiah, who follow the Lord with all
their hearts.

Being prosperous does not mean we will not have battles
to fight. For example, our finances and health are often on
the front lines against powerful enemies which shout words
of doubt and try to undermine faith in God's power to
provide for us. Our debts cry out, "You will never pay me in
full; I will only become a bigger burden to you." Illness and
weakness in our flesh scream, "Where is your God? I will take
you down, and you will not see another good day."

The king of Assyria came to fight against Hezekiah, king
of Judah, and had this message called out to the people of
Jerusalem from before the wall of the city, saying, "Is your
God able to deliver you from me?"

> Then the LORD sent an angel who cut down every
> mighty man of valor, leader, and captain in the camp of
> the king of Assyria. So he returned shamefaced to his own
> land. (2 Chron. 32:21)

My God is able to deliver and provide for me! He has
already paid the greatest debt for me and all mankind—sin's
debt—with the blood of His own Son. The flesh of my Lord
was torn for my frailty. His Word stands forever and will not
fail; it is true, and we can put our faith in it. *Thank You, my
Lord and King! You are my prosperity.*

8
Fellowship with God
✠

He who dwells in the secret place of the Most
High shall abide under the shadow of the
Almighty. I will say of the LORD,
"He is my refuge and my fortress;
My God, in Him I will trust."
(Psalms 91:1-2)

Fear and peace are opposites;
They will never come together,
You must leave fear behind
To come to peace.

Draw Me, Lord!

I have learned something that has made a big difference in my spiritual life. I have come to realize that I cannot come on my own into the relationship with God that I desire; as much as I want to have the desire for God, I cannot initiate it within myself.

From a child I have sung songs with lines such as "Draw me nearer Lord, nearer blessed Lord." I have prayed similar prayers, yet always there was a mind set that following God was up to me, and I had to do it all. Of course, I was unable to reach high enough in my own ability. God, in His mercy, reached down to me.

My deep, heart-felt prayer continually now is this: *Draw me, Lord! Draw me to You; I cannot reach You; I will not get to You unless You draw me.* He will and He does draw me to Himself. I spent a lot of years trying to reach that place in God through my own strength and willpower, depending on myself to make the relationship work through my prayers, my faithfulness, and my devotion. I do not mean to minimize any of these things, but there was one thing that I did not consider: God's desire to draw me to Himself. Millions of people want to walk with God; why would God care for one like me? He does care! He desires to draw me to Himself even more than I desire to be drawn.

If you see your fellowship with God fading, and your weakness looms large in your mind, look up and pray, "Draw me Lord!" All He is waiting for is for you to call, and He will be at your side. He cares for you! He has pledged Himself to His bride, and he will not give up on His beloved.

I am my beloved's, and his desire is toward me.
(Song 7:10)

Draw near to my soul, and redeem it; deliver me because of my enemies. (Ps. 69:18)

"Because he has set his love upon Me, therefore I will deliver him; I will set him on high, because he has known My name. He shall call upon Me, and I will answer him; I will be with him in trouble; I will deliver him and honor him." (Ps. 91:14-15)

"The LORD did not set His love on you nor choose you because you were more in number than any other people, for you were the least of all peoples; but because the LORD loves you, and because He would keep the oath which He swore to your fathers, the LORD has brought you out with a mighty hand, and redeemed you from the house of bondage, from the hand of Pharaoh king of Egypt." (Deut. 7:7-8)

When we pledge our lives and our love to Jesus, He pledges His love to us. He loved us and gave His life for us before we even knew Him!

Balance

A thought has been incubating in my mind for some weeks now, and I want to try to put it on paper. I admit I am spiritually weak in some areas, and this question arises: "Is it weakness that makes me strong, or is it weakness that brings me to the point of destruction?" It is my weakness that makes me cling more tightly than ever to God, but it is also that same weakness that causes me to turn from God. I want to live a contented life with my Lord, knowing He is my only strength. When I see my own strength, I tend to look down on my fellow man; when I see my own weakness, I can only look up to God. Is my weakness good for my spiritual man because it makes me look honestly at myself and others? It is not good in itself, but the good comes in how I respond to it. Weakness makes me look up to God for hope, and reach out to others with compassion. Should I then accept my weakness and let it remain? No—a thousand times, no! I must reach higher, I must grow stronger, and I must do better. Will I then become proud of myself, stop looking up to my Maker, and begin treating my fellow man with disdain?

It is as if I am a tight-rope walker, continually balancing from the beginning to the end of the walk. So easily I could fall to my death on one side because of weakness, or on the other side because of pride.

What conclusion do I draw? I must trust in God to save my soul from sin on a minute-by-minute basis, realizing I am only as good as who I am in Him. When I fall, I must reach my hand up to Him; when I am strong, I must reach my hand out to my fellows with all the love and compassion that Jesus extends to me every minute.

O Lord, I am a man that lives by faith, not by strength, nor by goodness in me. I depend on You every second for my breath of life. You never fail me. Day by day, You are continually giving me transfusions of Your life-saving blood. Without Your blood, Lord, the raging infection of sin all around me would bring me quickly to the point of death. Only You are holy, and Your mercy endures forever.

I will not fret over what I am, for I am what I am in Him, and that is all I am. If I think there is more than what my Lord provides, I fool myself; if I think there is less than I need, I turn my back on His grace.

I will not live at peace with my sin, nor will I live in fear of sin. There is no peace in fear. In His love there is life and peace; by His grace, there I will stay.

He who dwells in the secret place of the Most High shall abide under the shadow of the Almighty. I will say of the LORD, "He is my refuge and my fortress; My God, in Him I will trust." (Ps. 91:1-2)

Journey to the Mountaintop

Lord, why do I struggle to come into Your presence?
I suppose it is not the coming that I struggle with;
It is my feeling of Your presence.
All Your peace, love, and joy —
This is what I long to obtain.

I keep looking for formulas
That will get me into the awe of Your glory,
But none of my contrived formulas work consistently.
It takes time, but it is not the time itself,
Or the way I pray,
Or the discipline to put myself in the right frame of mind;
No one particular method will work every time.
What is the essence of what I need?

"Love Me unreservedly, and no other."

Yes, that is the answer!
But why is my love for You so often flawed and impure?
No matter how I try,
I cannot find all the flaws and impurities;
Those I do see stick to me like glue and I cannot cast them away.

"That for which you have not worked will be of little
Value to you."

Why must it be that way?

"When all is perfect between you and your wife,
Do you spend as much time courting and wooing her?
No, you begin to take her for granted,
And you drift apart.
It is the effort that makes the joy so great.

If you lived on the mountaintop,
The view would soon become normal and plain to you.
When you and I meet,
It is the toil of the climb
That makes the mountaintop so sweet."

Lord, What Do You Desire for Me?

"Don't be so busy.
Care more about your brother.
Take pleasure in the little blessings I give you every day.
Hear the song of a bird, and feel the gentle breeze.
Think of Me.

Don't be afraid to ask Me the hard questions;
Take time to hear the answers.
Join yourself to your brother;
He will fail you as often as you fail me;
I still love you; love him still.

Laugh with Me, cry with Me;
Tell Me about your day.
Tell Me what hurts, what makes you smile.
Isn't this what friends do?

We are friends—you and I and your brother.
Be one with Me and one with your brother.
What you can't do, maybe your brother can;
What neither can do, I can.

You and I and your brother —
The three of us are a team.
We can join to the task in countless ways,
Over the entire world, for I am everywhere.
Any one of 100 million brothers and sisters
Are joined with us."

I asked the Lord a question, as I often do.
This was His answer, which I wrote without a pause.
He spoke to me with such love and kindness!
You must hear these words, too!

Finding Peace

What is peace? Peace is harmony among men, and harmony between God and each man, along with the rest and contentment that comes with that harmony.

Is it possible to have peace in your life all the time? Would it be good for you to have peace in your life all the time? In John 15:1-17 we find the answers to these questions about peace. Pay close attention to the word *abide,* which means to stay in a given place or relationship. This abiding is a harmonious relationship between you and Jesus and brings many blessings in addition to peace.

God's people are meant to live with inner peace, though there may be outward conflict. There can be peace in the middle of the worst circumstances if we abide in Jesus. He is my peace and the rest for my soul. The peace of God is more important to me than the breath of my physical body; it is the breath of life to my spiritual man. Without His peace, there is really no free joyous life.

There have been occasions in my life when I lived in God's peace for a while, but then along came something that stole it from me. I asked this question: "How do we keep ourselves in the peace of God?" I want to tell you about five points that I have seen in my life as important to maintaining the peace of God.

I. Bow down before God

Bow down before Him, your Mighty God. Spend time at His feet every day, not just occasionally. Do you want His peace and direction just sometimes, or all the time? He is the only one who always knows how to remove that hook you feel in your mind that is yanking you around and destroying your peace. Stay before Him until the peace comes.

"Come to Me, all you who labor and are heavy laden, and I will give you rest" (Matt. 11:28).

II. Write down notes from prayer times

When you meet with the Lord, write down notes about the experience. Keep minutes, if you will, of your prayer meeting. Many of the things I have written came directly from my prayer notebook or were inspired by those notes. If you were at a very important business meeting that affected the lives and destiny of you and your family, wouldn't you want to take a few notes? Your time spent with God is more important than any meeting you will ever have in this world. If you take the time to write down what you have learned, you lock in the gains you have made. It is good to go back and read from your notes what you heard and learned from God.

> Whatever you have learned or received or heard from me, or seen in me—put it into practice. And the God of peace will be with you. (Phil. 4:9 NIV)

III. Lay down hindrances

Give up the thing that blocks the peace of God. Hindrances take all kinds of forms, some of which are anger, worry, fear, pride, the drive to be perfect, or that important thing that you must do. Your concern about things people expect you to do, or who they expect you to be can also become a block to peace. Give it up and walk away.

You may think, "I do not want to lay down my anger; I deserve to be angry." (Anger and peace cannot dwell in the same house.)

Or you may ask, "Who will worry about it, if I don't?" (If you can solve a problem, do it; but worrying never solved a problem, and never will.)

Maybe you say, "The solution to my situation seems impossible! Why shouldn't I be afraid?"
(Fear and peace are opposites; they will never come together, so you must leave fear behind to come to peace.)

"Doesn't God expect us to be perfect?" you may ask. (No, He does not expect us to be perfect; He wants our fellowship with Him to be perfect, and in that fellowship He will perfect us.)

"What I am doing is important, and people depend on me," you insist. (If it is truly a job that you must do, God will give you the grace and peace to do it, but so many times we do not have our priorities in order, or we do things for the wrong reasons.)

God has a ministry, maybe several ministries, for each of us to do. When God has anointed you for ministry, He will give you a desire and a love for it. I once asked a dear friend how he felt about what I thought was his ministry, and his answer was something like this: "I love it; it makes me feel useful; it is the only time I feel truly fulfilled, and I don't want it to end."

Sometimes, I have lost my peace because I was trying to do things that I hated doing simply because I thought, "Somebody has to do it."

If you feel a desire to try something new, do it. Maybe God is building that desire in your life. Don't worry about whether or not you think you are able to do it. If you are acting on a God-given desire for a ministry, God will pour ten times more ability through you to do the work than the most talented person who is depending on his own ability.

The peace of God, which surpasses all understanding, will guard your hearts and minds through Christ Jesus. (Phil. 4:7)

IV. Set down heavy loads

Maybe you have a God-given, "important" ministry and you love doing it, but the job has gotten too heavy for you. You keep plugging on, even though you find yourself spinning your wheels and going nowhere. You keep going on because you know this is the job you are meant to do, only now you are not doing it because you love it, but because you are supposed to do it. Somewhere amid the cares of life you have lost the zeal for the Lord's work that once was so important in your life.

Throw it down and walk away for awhile! Don't try to just go through the motions; lay it down completely for an hour, a day, a week, a month, or a year, whatever time it takes to get your peace about it restored. I am not telling you to give up and quit, but just to take a vacation from your tasks. Go somewhere and get your bearings. Don't worry; "your job" in the church can wait. Do you think God's plan is going to fail if you are away from your post for a little while? Love what you do, but don't work at it until it kills you. Realize that you are not indispensable; the church will not die while you rest awhile.

> Now may the Lord of peace Himself give you peace always in every way. The Lord be with you all. (2 Thess. 3:16)

V. Get deep into the Word

Often, we are too shallow in our Bible study. We must get deep into the Word of God. It is great when the words just jump off the page and thrill our souls. Other times, we read a portion of scripture and immediately know deep down in our spirits that there is something more to be learned. This is the treasure detector of the Holy Spirit at work saying, "Dig; there is treasure here." Don't just underline it and think, "This is interesting." Dig! Some of the greatest treasures in life are the ones unearthed while digging in the Word, and they are also the ones that will stick in our minds and become a part of our lives.

> God is not the author of confusion but of peace. (1 Cor. 14:33)

9
Dig in the WORD!

Many books are full of golden nuggets mined by another from God's Holy Word, but these shiny treasures can never match the treasure gained by your own sweat and tears!

We can repeatedly hear the Word and think that we believe it, but the Word truly becomes part of us when we form the words with our own lips in faith.

Commandments with Purpose

> Now the purpose of the commandment is love from a
> pure heart, from a good conscience, and from sincere
> faith. (1 Tim. 1:5)

If we had our way, there would not be any rules, and we
would do only the things pleasing to us. In His wisdom and
love for us, God has given us commandments for a reason;
they are not just arbitrary.

Love is the purpose of the commandments, because love is the
highest attribute of God. Love is more than just kindness and
goodness. It compels the lover to give all of himself for the
object of his love. First Corinthians chapter thirteen gives us
a detailed description of this love.

The heart is the center and depth of our being. Love from
a *pure heart* signifies that this heart has one primary purpose,
one motive, and one object; it is not diluted or mixed with
other goals. If we say we love God but continue to live in our
own stubborn way, not obeying His commandments, we walk
not in love, but hypocrisy.

A *good conscience* toward God is the skeleton that gives our
frail flesh the ability to raise its face to the one we love. If we
are walking with our Master in all the light He has given us,
then we will enjoy a wonderful, loving fellowship with Him.

Faith reaches far beyond what we can see and even what
we can understand. If we couple genuine, sincere faith with
the love beyond understanding that God has for us, then
what we get is too big for words, too deep for tears, and
beyond the scope of happiness; it is a love that is joy
unspeakable and full of glory.

What Is Love?

Read I Corinthians, chapter thirteen.

Love is the sum of all it means to be godly. Our tendency is to give up on people when they don't meet our expectations, or when they are displeasing to us, but love is patient and long-suffering. It is a rare person that does not have a mental stopping point; in other words, "My love for you will stop if this or that happens." Pull out all the stops and let the Holy Spirit work into your life an open-ended love, without restraints.

It is so easy to get angry at another's faults and push them away, but love reaches out a gentle hand of kindness. Though it is hard for us, by the grace of God we can reach out in kindness when all our human reason says that we have a right to be angry.

Human nature asks, "Why is he blessed and I am not? Why does he always get the good and I get the rotten?" Love, on the other hand, is glad when others are blessed. Open your hands and release the desire to grasp what pleases only you and look for what is also pleasing to others; let your heart be glad that blessings are there for your brother.

Love will not blow up into selfish anger, bringing up all the past failures and sins when it does not get its way. Love is not glad when a brother fails, saying, "I told you so," but in humility, it hopes, expects, and believes the very best. God has forgotten our sins; Lord, help us to forget our brother's sins.

Love is a commitment, not a feeling, so it does not give up, no matter how long it takes and through whatever circumstance, until God's purpose is fulfilled.

God is love, and he who abides in love abides in God, and God in him. (1 John 4:16)

Three Goals

Blessed are they whose ways are blameless, who walk
according to the law of the LORD. Blessed are they who
keep his statutes and seek him with all their heart. They do
nothing wrong; they walk in his ways. (Ps. 119:1-3 NIV)

We see in this scripture three goals for us to strive
toward: (1) To travel the journey here on Earth in a way that
is blameless—live a life with no regrets. (2) To keep His
statutes—in other words, do all as Jesus would do it. (3) To
do nothing wrong—live a life without sin.

This scripture shows us the way to accomplish each goal:
(1) If we want to live our lives with no regrets, then we
should walk in God's law. We cannot make up our own plan
on how to live an untarnished life; we must go to the Bible.
The Word is meant to be obeyed, not just read. God made
the rules. We follow them. He will make our lives count for
good if we do it His way. (2) If we want to do things just as
Jesus would do them, then we should seek Him with all our
heart. We do not know how to do things as He would unless
we do whatever it takes to find His way. (3) If we want to live
a life without sin, then we should "walk in His ways," living
continually in fellowship with Him. A quick prayer here and a
quick Bible verse there will not suffice; it takes total
commitment to walk in His ways. In case you have not gotten
the point already, the most important thought I want to
convey to the readers of this book is this: Set aside time in a
quiet place to spend with the Lord in prayer and reading of
His Word every day!

I believe that for everything our Lord expects of us, He
shows us over and over again just exactly how to accomplish
it in our lives.

Hidden in My Heart

I have hidden your word in my heart that I might not sin against you. Praise be to you, O LORD; teach me your decrees. With my lips I recount all the laws that come from your mouth. (Ps. 119:11-13 NIV)

Though the word *hidden* can mean out of sight and out of mind, in this verse that is not the meaning at all. The Word being hidden in the heart is like bricks that are hidden in a brick wall; the bricks of the Word, the building material to build a good heart, are hidden in plain sight. Everywhere in the heart that we focus our thoughts, we should see another brick, whether it is a word of encouragement or a word of warning.

I don't suppose I will ever have enough of the Word hidden in my heart. When I had been downcast with some heavy troubles for a couple of days, I was reminded by a wise daughter to look back to the Word, which I did; then I felt rejuvenated in spirit.

In the early years of America, the Bible was used as a teaching tool. It was read in schools and quoted in public forums. People used biblical terminology in everyday life. We have lost even this basic biblical background, so we must work doubly hard to fill our minds with the Word of God.

When our hearts are filled with God's Word, it will flow from us. *Lord, let Your words flow like a river into me and out of me.* We can repeatedly hear the Word and think that we believe it, but the Word truly becomes part of us when we form the words with our own lips in faith.

A Soul after God

My soul is consumed with longing for your laws at all times. You rebuke the arrogant, who are cursed and who stray from your commands. Remove from me scorn and contempt, for I keep your statutes. (Ps. 119:20-22 NIV)

The psalmist begins by saying, "My whole being is filled with a hunger to find Your perfect Word being accomplished in my life at all times." I try to put these words in my mouth, and I must admit they are not a perfect fit. Yet I do desire that my soul be broken with a yearning to always walk in God's perfect plan. With what am I consumed in my daily life? For what does my heart long? It is too often not the Word of God.

The Lord truly knows what is in the heart. Either we are with those who long for Him, or we are with the proud and arrogant who stray from His Word and are cursed. We try to put ourselves in that gray area in-between, but there is no in-between; we will be on one side or the other.

Feeling our inadequacy, we begin to judge ourselves and ask, "How can I be what a holy God desires me to be?" God does not see us as we see ourselves. He declared Abraham righteous because of his faith. "For by grace are ye saved through faith; and that not of yourselves: it is the gift of God:" (Eph. 2:8 KJV).

We may feel scorn and contempt because of our own weakness and the criticism of others. Nevertheless, trust in God's Word and His love, and He will show you the right way. I have seen people fall away from God because they found themselves unable to live a perfect life. Then others, like David, were clearly imperfect in many ways, yet they continued to follow God to the best of their ability. It is not perfect deeds that God desires of us, but perfect faith that keeps us charging forward with our eyes always on Him.

Doorkeeper

Better is one day in your courts than a thousand elsewhere;
I would rather be a doorkeeper in the house of my God
than dwell in the tents of the wicked. For the LORD God
is a sun and shield; the LORD bestows favor and honor; no
good thing does he withhold from those whose walk is
blameless. (Ps. 84:10-11 NIV)

One good day, one really good day, is when I know I am
doing the right thing and am in the right place with a right
heart. When I lay my head down at night, there is that sweet
knowledge that all is well with my soul.

What does a doorkeeper do? He stations himself near the
door and watches closely all who enter or leave. He is always
alert to any need that should be taken care of for the good of
the household. Even the doorkeeper in God's house is a
position of great importance. There is no unimportant job in
God's Kingdom. Most all the people of the world are running
as hard as they can through the door of the tent of
wickedness, trying to grab all they can get for themselves and
seeking all the pleasure they can enjoy. On the other hand,
the doorkeeper in God's house is there to serve, to do what is
needed for someone else, with no thought for himself. He
always stands in the light of God's presence and under the
protection of His mighty hand. This doorkeeper doesn't look
for men's recognition, but is honored to wear a uniform—a
robe of righteousness dipped in blood—given to him by
Jesus Christ.

Where is God's house? It is all over the world, wherever
the Spirit of God leads you.

Walk blamelessly before Him!

Don't Walk, Stand, or Sit; Run!

> Blessed is the man who does not walk in the counsel of
> the wicked or stand in the way of sinners or sit in the seat
> of mockers. (Ps. 1:1 NIV)

From where does the counsel of the ungodly come? It
comes from those who are not following God. At an ever-
increasing rate, through TV, radio, newspapers, magazines,
internet, billboards, mail, and books, we are told to follow our
own way. If we would walk after God, we must choose to
hear His counsel, or else the ungodly counsel that is
screaming at us from every direction will cause us to deviate
from the path of righteousness.

How do we hear His counsel? We must spend time with
Him. Ungodly counsel may masquerade as good, telling us
things such as, "You don't have time; God understands you
have to get to work to provide for your family and care for
your children," or "You can't miss that important
appointment," or "There is housework to do." The list of
mostly good things grows longer and becomes more evil as
we drift farther and farther away from our time with God.
We cannot stop ungodly influences, but we can get away to a
secret place with God, talk to Him, and more importantly,
listen to Him.

Have you ever just stopped at a crossroads and
looked down the road other than the one you are traveling,
wondering what was further down that other road? We
cannot avoid crossing paths with sinners, but if we stop and
consider the sinner's path even for a moment, we will be
drawn by something pleasing. The longer we stand there, the
stronger the pull of that path will become, until before we
know what is happening, we are taking a few steps down the
path to see what is around the bend in the road. We stretch
our necks to see, but we can't quite see all we want to see, so
we take a few more steps down the path. After a short time,

the path becomes comfortable and we enjoy the scenery. Maybe we say we will never follow the sinner's path, but will just cross his path as often as possible, catching a glimpse while crossing. Instead of hurrying across the path, our pace gets slower and slower as we cross in order to see as much as possible as we go by.

If we stand in the path of sinners we will begin to listen to the counsel of the ungodly people who are traveling on that path; then we will find ourselves beginning to think, talk, and act like them. Are we sitting there on our couches watching when TV comics make fun of God and all that is godly? Do we then find ourselves talking and acting in the same ways?

If you have listened to and followed the counsel of the ungodly and stopped to stand in the path of sinners, then the next step is to go down the path and find a comfortable spot where you can sit down. When someone sits down, he is planning to stay for a while. Now you have become one of those voices of ungodly counsel that is calling to your brethren to follow you down the path of sin.

Blessed is the man who keeps on running into God's presence.

> The name of the LORD is a strong tower; the righteous run
> to it and are safe. (Prov. 18:10 NIV)

The Best Kind of Bible Study

The best kind of Bible study is independent Bible study. This means studying on your own without the help of commentaries and reference books, using only your Bible and a concordance with Hebrew and Greek dictionaries. After a thorough study, then check your work with commentaries. This type of study will help you to learn more, give you better understanding, and help you to longer retain what you have learned. Also, this method will help you overcome the prejudice and preconceived ideas inherent in any commentary or reference book. This independent study must be soaked in prayer and guided by the Holy Spirit, for without His anointing we study in vain.

Bible study must be more than just praying and expecting the Holy Spirit to dump all knowledge into your brain; the Lord will give you plenty of water, but you have to dig the well. You might say, "With all the great Bible knowledge found in so many good books, why not just study another person's book?" The answer is simple: the man who digs the well will enjoy the water much more than the stranger who just gets a drink in passing and forgets about the well. If you go to all the trouble of digging a well, you will certainly take the time to guard the well and keep it flowing.

Pastors and teachers can teach us much that we need to know about the Bible, but second-hand knowledge is never as good as first-hand knowledge; besides, we need to make sure that what we are taught is the truth.

The truth of the Bible is spiritual, so only those spiritually qualified can understand it adequately.

[Qualities needed: A new heart - (1 Corinthians 2:14), A hungry heart - (1 Peter 2:2), An obedient heart - (Psalms 119:98), A disciplined heart - (Matthew 7:7), A teachable heart - (Isaiah 50:4)].[1]

1. T. Norton Sterrett, *How To Understand Your Bible* . (InterVarsity Press, Downers Grove, 1978) 19-21.

A New Song of Praise

Praise the LORD! Sing to the LORD a new song, and His praise in the assembly of saints. Let Israel rejoice in their Maker; let the children of Zion be joyful in their King. (Ps. 149:1-2)

The last five chapters of the book of Psalms start with the words "Praise the LORD." Wouldn't you say that it must be important to praise Him? The word *praise* comes from a Latin word meaning *value* or *price*; so, when we give praise to God, we proclaim His worthiness. What is He worth to me today?

What is a song? It is a combination of beautiful harmonious sounds. It is poetic words set to music. It is words from the heart expressed with emotion. In this verse, the psalmist admonishes us to sing a new song and to sing His praise.

Why sing a new song? I believe God wants to hear from our lips the praise that is in our own hearts for Him now, this very minute. You can know you are loved, but there is nothing so good, even grand, than to hear that heartfelt expression of love in another person's spoken words.

I encourage you children to praise, rejoice, and be joyful in the presence of your King. Let that song bubble up from the depths of your soul; it will cause you to see how big your God really is, and how little your problem has always been.

As I write this, while also listening to my *Opening Windows* CD, I just now hear, "We don't worship God to change God, we worship God to change us."[2]

From a heart that loves God, sing your song—a new song, a true song—a song that lifts Him up and directs hearts to Him.

---

2. Max Lucado, *Opening Windows*, Glenn Wagner, (Here to Him Music, 1998).

Do Not Withhold Good

> Do not withhold good from those to whom it is due, when
> it is in the power of your hand to do so. Do not say to
> your neighbor, "Go, and come back, and tomorrow I will
> give it," When you have it with you. (Prov. 3:27-28)

Am I withholding good from anyone to whom it is due?
When I think about that for a while, I begin to think of all the
good things that have been done for me that I did not
deserve. It is God's nature to give good things to his family,
even to the prodigal, whom He would desire to bring to
Himself. We might interpret "to whom it is due" as those to
whom wages are due for the good work they did. I am so glad
God did not give me only my wages; I'm sure they would be
small. God gives to us generously when we need it. I look
back ashamedly at the times I have passed by when I saw
someone in need of something that I could have provided.
Don't make the same mistake in your lives. If it is in your
power to meet a need, meet it; however, don't let guilt be a
rod upon your back if it is not really in your power to help.
Do what you can, when you can do it wisely and safely.

Remember that obedience is better than sacrifice. At
times I have said to myself, "I will make up for it later," when
I knew I had with me the thing that would meet a specific
need. Sometimes we make sacrifices trying to atone for past
disobedience to this scripture, but more often we say,
"someone else will meet the need," when it is perfectly in our
power to meet our neighbor's need.

We are able to give to whom it is due because of God's
gift of good to us. He gave what He had with Him—His only
Son!

Established by the Lord

The steps of a good man are ordered by the LORD, and He delights in his way. Though he fall, he shall not be utterly cast down; for the LORD upholds him with His hand. I have been young, and now am old; yet I have not seen the righteous forsaken, nor his descendants begging bread. He is ever merciful, and lends; and his descendants are blessed. (Ps. 37:23-26)

My steps are established by the Lord. He can work in ways I could never dream of and give strength that I could never have within myself. When He has established my way, then He can delight in it, for it is a way He has laid out for me.

Surprisingly, this scripture does not say *if* he falls, but *when* he falls. Though I will fall sometimes, Father is holding my hand, and He will catch me just in time. Even if I'm dangling over the Grand Canyon, He's got a firm grip on my hand. I'm sure glad I don't have to depend on my feeble grip and think that I am the one holding on. Hanging there by my hand, when I look down, I'm terrified; but when I look up into His eyes, fear melts away and all is right with my soul. He never loses His grip, even when I lose mine. If God holds my hand, all the worst things I can face in life, as horrible as they may be, will seem to be but a skinned knee when viewed in the course of eternity.

I feel like I have laid claim to the Psalmist's words. God has never forsaken me or my family; He is the one who always provides for us. I know that many hard trials and struggles may come, but I also know that God is always there holding my hand.

Lord, help me to follow Your example, to be gracious, and to give of myself. Please cause my children to be a blessing always.

Because You Have Obeyed

"Will you not receive instruction to obey My words?" says the LORD. "The words of Jonadab the son of Rechab, which he commanded his sons, not to drink wine, are performed; for to this day they drink none, and obey their father's commandment. But although I have spoken to you, rising early and speaking, you did not obey Me." (Jer. 35:13-14)

And Jeremiah said to the house of the Rechabites, "Thus says the LORD of hosts, the God of Israel: 'Because you have obeyed the commandment of Jonadab your father, and kept all his precepts and done according to all that he commanded you, therefore thus says the LORD of hosts, the God of Israel: "Jonadab the son of Rechab shall not lack a man to stand before Me forever." ' " (Jer 35:18-19)

God honors obedience to the authority that He has set over us. Even more so, He expects us to obey His instructions. We see in these verses that God gave a promise to a family who had been obedient to a wise father, even after his death. This promise will astound you when you consider it: there will never be a time when a descendant of Jonadab, the son of Rechab, will not be standing before God. Always is a long time. When we walk the streets of heaven, we will see Rechabites. What really excites me is the fact that (I believe) down through all the ages, these thousands of years since Jeremiah's time, descendants of these same Rechabites have always been on earth serving God.

We do not live only for ourselves, but all that we say and do influences others in one way or another. We affect our children and all those around us for good or for evil. I want to always be a "Rechabite" influence on others and to see you stand before God always because you have obeyed His Word.

Focus on Jesus

"Therefore I say to you, do not worry about your life, what you will eat or what you will drink; nor about your body, what you will put on. Is not life more than food and the body more than clothing? Look at the birds of the air, for they neither sow nor reap nor gather into barns; yet your heavenly Father feeds them. Are you not of more value than they?" (Matt. 6:25-26)

Why on earth do we fret so often about things like food and clothing? These are basic necessities that we all must have daily, but they are not the most important part of our lives. What or who is our treasure? If Jesus Christ is the shelter of our souls, if being in His presence is our sustenance, then we have no need to worry about anything. "For where your treasure is, there your heart will be also" (Matt. 6:21).

Upon what are your spiritual eyes focused? If your focus is on Him, all is well. I'm reminded of the old song "It Is Well with My Soul" that was penned after the author lost his family in a shipwreck; his eyes were on the Lord and all was well. "The lamp of the body is the eye. If therefore your eye is good, your whole body will be full of light" (Matt. 6:22).

It is so easy to get anxious and worried about all the situations in our lives. Remember that Jesus sees the circumstances of every little sparrow, and He says we are worth much more to Him than many sparrows. Don't fret! God always has everything under control for the good of His kingdom and for all those who are part of His kingdom.

Seek the Kingdom; Don't Worry

"But seek first the kingdom of God and His righteousness,
and all these things shall be added to you. Therefore do
not worry about tomorrow, for tomorrow will worry about
its own things. Sufficient for the day is its own trouble."
(Matt. 6:33-34)

Jesus teaches us in this scripture to seek the kingdom and
refrain from worry. It is all a matter of what thoughts you
allow to dominate your mind, and what things you pursue
with all your energy. If you use your intellect and energy
seeking only material things and pleasures of this life, then
you will be full of worry and will be fretting all the time,
because you can't force things to be just as your dreams
would paint them. Instead, you could say, "How can I turn
loose of what I want in this life and accept God's provision?"
Forcing your desires out of your mind without filling it with
something else will only create a vacuum; those desires will
just flood back as fast as you force them out. Did you ever try
to force the air out of a bottle? How did you do it? That's
right!—You filled it with something else, like water or milk.
Jesus did not say stop worrying first and then seek the
kingdom, but He said seek the kingdom first. As we pour our
mental and physical energy into seeking God, worry will be
replaced with faith. You can then believe that He cares about
what you need.

Trust God to know what you really need, and to provide
in His way and in His time. The Spirit directs your prayers,
bringing them into agreement with His will, so that according
to His timing, His plan is accomplished in your life.

We are most always focused on one tiny segment of the
life before us, while God sees all our future. Don't fret about
the future; it is firmly held in God's all-powerful hands.

Be Separate

Therefore "Come out from among them and be separate, says the Lord. Do not touch what is unclean, and I will receive you. I will be a Father to you, and you shall be My sons and daughters, says the LORD Almighty." (2 Cor. 6:17-18)

Therefore, having these promises, beloved, let us cleanse ourselves from all filthiness of the flesh and spirit, perfecting holiness in the fear of God. (2 Cor. 7:1)

Do we want to be children of the Father or children of the flesh? Do we want to be welcomed by the world or welcomed by God? We must be separate from the world to be near to God. We have choices and promises; if we make the right choice, the promises are surely ours. Our irrevocable guarantee is in these words: "Says the LORD Almighty."

Paul is saying, "We have the plan and we have the promises; let us get to work, children." The Bible puts things so simply, but we keep muddying the water with our desire to do things our way. What we cling to is what rules our lives. Will it be the world, or will it be God?

Time after time, I have had to learn this lesson—a lesson that is so simple—"Give everything to God." I have gripped ever so tightly to something and did not want to turn loose, or more often, thought I could not turn loose. Then I felt such freedom when God at last brought me to the place of willingness to lay it His feet. This is a lesson that we must learn and re-learn in countless ways throughout life. Be a quick learner; it will save you much labor.

Value Added

While reading the first few chapters of I Chronicles today, I began to question the reason for all the genealogies in the Bible. One word that comes to mind is *connected*. We are all connected to someone who lived before us and someone who will live after us. The body carries the DNA which plays an important part in the quirks, strengths, and weaknesses that make us who we are. Also, our thoughts and actions reflect what we were taught by others, whether consciously or unconsciously.

Each of us is a creation of God through a man and a woman. Our goal should be to preserve the best from the past generation, add value to it, and pass it on to the future generation. This cannot be done simply by the wisdom of mankind; it is only accomplished by the work of the Holy Spirit in us. If we pass on only the DNA we received, we do nothing but pass on the sins of Adam to a new generation; but if we pass on a spiritual heritage to our children, we show them the way to be delivered from the sins of Adam.

Those who are foolish and selfish would like to deny this connection, because without it they feel free to do as they wish, with no regard to anyone else. Nevertheless, all that we are and all that we do affects, in some way, those around us. Men cannot flippantly throw away what thousands of generations have proved to be true and right without bringing great harm to themselves and those that come after them. We are all connected, whether we like it or not.

> The way of a fool seems right to him, but a wise man listens to advice. (Prov. 12:15 NIV)

Great value can only be added to this human connection from the past to the future if we are joined through God and His Word. Even if what was passed on to us was of little or no value, there is still hope in God; He can make us brand new.

> Therefore, if anyone is in Christ, he is a new creation; the old has gone, the new has come! (2 Cor. 5:17 NIV)

In the genealogy recorded in I Chronicles, there was a man of the family of Judah whose name was Jabez. His name, which means "he will cause pain," was given to him by his mother because she bore him with much pain. Jabez became an honorable man and turned to God. He asked five things from God:

> And Jabez called on the God of Israel saying, "Oh, that You would bless me indeed, and enlarge my territory, that Your hand would be with me, and that You would keep me from evil, that I may not cause pain!" (1 Chron. 4:10)

The Bible simply says God granted to him what he asked.

Live your life for God. Like Jabez, ask of His blessings, let Him direct your path in life, and be thankful for what He gives you. As you live in fellowship with God, you will not cause pain to others, but you will be a blessing and will add value to the lives of continuing generations.

Weapons of War

> For though we walk in the flesh, we do not war according
> to the flesh. For the weapons of our warfare are not carnal
> but mighty in God for pulling down strongholds, casting
> down arguments and every high thing that exalts itself
> against the knowledge of God, bringing every thought into
> captivity to the obedience of Christ. (2 Cor. 10:3-5)

It is hard to grasp the meaning of *not warring according to the
flesh*. We live our lives in this flesh, but we cannot use physical
weapons to fight against the enemy of the soul.

What are the weapons that are going to pull down
strongholds? We first need to see where these strongholds
are. They are in the hearts and minds of men. Only God can
get into the arena where this battle is fought, so our weapons
must be God-empowered weapons. What weapons can be
used against the arguments instigated by the enemy? Might it
be first the Word of God, and then the Spirit-directed word
of wisdom? What will knock down arrogance of the mind
that causes men to think they are smarter than God? The
Spirit of God working in and through a yielded vessel of clay
will confound the self-appointed wise men of this world. As
we allow the Word of God to fill our minds, we can bring our
thoughts into obedience to the Lord, thus displacing the
thoughts of the flesh. The Word says "Pray without ceasing"
(1 Thess. 5:17). "Thy word have I hid in mine heart, that I
might not sin against thee" (Ps. 119:11 KJV).

Our ammunition to use in the war against the enemy of
our souls comes from scripture, and the firepower comes
from the indwelling Holy Spirit who guides us and who
knows how to use the spiritual weapons. In any battle,
weapons must be reloaded. By spending time in the Word
and in prayer daily, we are renewed for the battle.

Anxious

> Be anxious for nothing, but in everything by prayer and supplication, with thanksgiving, let your requests be made known to God; and the peace of God, which surpasses all understanding, will guard your hearts and minds through Christ Jesus. (Phil. 4:6-7)

Why should you get all bothered about things that you cannot control? When you feel anxiousness boiling up, just let the air out of it by crying out to the Maker of all things. He made you, didn't He? He can and will work out the problem, and do it well every time.

You should understand prayer by now, but what about that big word *supplication*? What does it mean? Well, it's quite simple. It's explaining to God in your prayers exactly what you need, getting very specific in your request about a need that is important to you. This is not so that God will understand your problem; it is to settle in your own mind, with words of faith, what you want and why you want it. Just stop and think about that for a minute or two. Here I am talking to my Father, the Maker of the universe, who knows all about this thing that is causing trouble for me.

I see this picture in my mind's eye of a big boulder in front of me, and then of God looking down from his vantage point and seeing this little speck of dust in His hand that only requires the slightest puff to blow it away. That's when I can start thanking Him and praising my awesome God.

We must make known to God what is bothering us, lay it all out before Him, and trust Him to deal with our specific need. We can have peace of mind when we realize we cannot solve our problems, but that God can and will, in His own way and in His own time. Our responsibility is to pray, trust, and never worry.

The Chamber of Time

What do we know about time? We know God made it. God lives in the eternal, where there is no difference in past, present, or future; it is all the same to Him. For us, God made time that we may use it to prepare to live in His realm. In Ecclesiastes 3:1-8, we see seven groups of four. Seven is God's number of completion,[1] and four is the number for earthly things,[2] so we see here seven aspects of the time we must complete here on earth.

We live our earthly lives according to time; it can be our friend or our enemy. When we are following closely after God, He makes time our friend. God is not in a hurry; He has plenty of time. When time gets in His way, He just puts it on hold. Often, I feel that time and I are in a war with each other. I think I do not have enough time to do what I want and need to do, or I am frustrated when I must spend time waiting, or I feel ashamed for wasting time. If time is all we have, then we are no better than the animals that live and die and go back to the earth, but God has given us something beyond time.

> He has made everything beautiful in its time. He has also set eternity in the hearts of men; yet they cannot fathom what God has done from beginning to end. (Eccl. 3:11 NIV).

> To everything there is a season, a time for every purpose under heaven. (Eccl. 3:1)

Let us, for a moment, think of time as a place built within God's eternity as a chamber for the bride of His Son. This chamber's purpose is for the preparation of the bride to meet her Husband in eternity.

We can observe these valuable preparations that the bride will make in her earthly chamber of time:

[1.] A time to be born, and a time to die; a time to plant, and a
time to pluck what is planted; (Eccl. 3:2).

She endures with patience her allotted time in the
chamber, knowing there is a wedding coming at the end of
her stay. As a young woman she thinks of her life as lasting
forever, with plenty of time to get around to everything, but
as she travels through this place called time, the end becomes
more apparent. She cannot choose when she checks into this
room of time, nor can she choose when she will leave, but
she can choose how she lives while she is there.

[2.] A time to kill, and a time to heal; a time to break down, and
a time to build up; (Eccl. 3:3).

She allows the Holy Spirit to put to death the evil nature
that cannot live in eternity, and she seeks His help to grow
the good fruit that she will carry with her on her wedding day.
There are walls of fear and doubt that must be pulled down
so that the good graces of God can enter. There are walls of
protection that must be made strong against armies of lust
and corruption.

[3.] A time to weep, and a time to laugh; a time to mourn, and
a time to dance; (Eccl. 3:4).

Tears, laughter, sadness, and rejoicing—all these
emotions are experienced by the bride in her chamber.

[4.] A time to cast away stones, and a time to gather stones; a
time to embrace, and a time to refrain from embracing;
(Eccl. 3:5).

She faces countless decisions in her preparation chamber.
Some things must be thrown away, and other things gathered.
Now, she will have occasions to hug friends and family; then,
she will be able to hug Him forever.

[5.] A time to gain, and a time to lose; a time to keep, and a time to throw away; (Eccl. 3:6).

She gains beauty as she communicates with her Lord. Her preparation is very costly, but she is willing to give up anything to be His. She learns that faith, hope, and love are priceless, and keeps them in her heart. She makes the hard decisions to throw away what will be worthless in eternity.

[6.] A time to tear, and a time to sew; a time to keep silence, and a time to speak; (Eccl. 3:7).

She tears out the old and sews in the new. Sometimes silent, sometimes exuberant, she is becoming a woman of wisdom, knowing just what is needed for every occasion.

[7.] A time to love, and a time to hate; a time of war, and a time of peace (Eccl. 3:8).

Her love for her betrothed and His family is growing, as is her hatred for evil. She has been through wars in her chamber of time, but has also experienced great peace as His love surrounded her. She cannot wait to meet her Lover in the Cathedral of Eternity, and thinks of His love every minute. She is ready to leave behind the evil and hateful things of this earthly chamber. Now she is prepared to walk into the peace of eternity to meet her Husband.

Time—what will you do with it? Will you allow it to become a tool in the hand of the Master to bless your life, or will you make it a weapon for your own destruction?

---

1. Frank M. Boyd, Studies in Revelation, (Berean School of the Bible, Springfield, MO., 1967), 15.
2. Ibid.,16.

10
God Has a Plan
✝

I will instruct you and teach you in the way you
should go; I will guide you with My eye.
(Psalms 32:8)

When we ask God for direction, more often than
not, what we hear from Him is just this:
"Put your foot there; take this one little step."

The Commitment of Rebekah

Rebekah said *I will* to the everyday, mundane task of carrying a water pot to the well. She said *I will* to the one who asked of her what she had in her hand to give, and she said *I will* to the need of a weary traveler's animals. She said *I will* to a long journey into a strange and unknown land to see the one who called for her. She said *I will* to the eternal vows of commitment to the one she loved. Her willingness to commit herself to each single task that was in her power to do drew her eternally into the record of the greatest story ever told, redemption's story.

The love story of Rebekah and Isaac, like the love story between Jesus and each Christian is told by commitments. This is not a story of attraction, of feeling, of pleasures, or even of happiness. It is a story of commitment, and this commitment does bring great joy and eternal happiness in the presence of our God.

We first dip into the wellspring of our souls and pour out all that is within us to our Lord; He invites us to leave all we have and all we know to come to Him. The journey is long; it lasts a lifetime. Our trip to the house of our Lord may not always be easy, but around countless campfires along the way we are able to commune with Him. I can imagine Rebekah's myriad of questions to Abraham's servant, questions such as: "What is my lord Isaac like? What kind of person is he? What are his favorite things to do? What makes him smile? What pleases him the most?" We must ask these same kinds of questions as we read God's Word and spend time daily in prayer.

Will we, like Rebekah, know our Lord when we see Him in the distance? "Rebekah looked in the distance and saw Isaac. She jumped off her camel and asked, 'Is that my lord?'" (Gen. 24:64-65). (My paraphrase)

The Wrong Direction

Do we sometimes ask God for direction under false pretenses? In chapter forty-two of Jeremiah, that is what the Israelites did. Judah had fallen to the Babylonians, and the governor who had been set up over the remnant of Israel had been murdered. The remaining Israelites came to Jeremiah to ask direction of God: "Pray for us to the LORD your God, for all this remnant (since we are left but a few of many, as you can see), that the LORD your God may show us the way in which we should walk and the thing we should do" (Jer. 42:2-3). "Whether it is pleasing or displeasing, we will obey the voice of the LORD" (Jer. 42:6). These Israelites had decided to go to Egypt; they were sure that it was what God would tell them to do. They thought it was logical for them to leave the land now controlled by their enemy, and thereby save their lives. They told Jeremiah to pray to "your God." Was God not "their God" at that point, or had they become gods unto themselves?

We sometimes pray for direction, but we do not listen when we receive an answer; we have our minds already made up. Why, then, do we bother to pray? Do we come to God to sanction our predetermined plans? If we go to God for direction, then do not follow His direction, doesn't that make us rebels? If we are in rebellion, have we chosen a new master? Will you be the master of your destiny, or will God be in charge? I had rather put my fate in God's hands any time; wouldn't you?

"The LORD has said concerning you, O remnant of Judah, 'Do not go to Egypt!' " (Jer. 42:19)

So they went to the land of Egypt, for they did not obey the voice of the LORD. (Jer. 43:7)

I Want

I want—these are the watch words of our modern age! Driven by the desire to get what *I want*, husband and wife work day and night. Children are neglected and marriages fail because what *I want* is the focus. Also, these two little words—*I want*—slip into the church.

Do we even care what God wants? If we would truly follow God, we must bring those two little words to the altar and lay them down. Yes, this is easier said than done; *I want* has become part of our character, our hopes, our dreams; it is always on our minds.

We like verses such as, "May He grant you according to your heart's desire, And fulfill all your purpose" (Ps. 20:4). We take it as a license to seek what we want. We forget that the word also says, "Delight yourself also in the LORD, and He shall give you the desires of your heart" (Ps. 37:4). I believe this verse implies that we come first as a blank slate, delighting only in Him; then He will put desires in our hearts that He wants us to have, and will also satisfy those desires.

Lord, I bring my wants to You. Chop them in little bits, throw away all that is worthless and keep only what is good; if there is no good at all in my wants, cast them all away and build a new set of wants in me so that what you want, I want. Then I do not have to fight for what I want, because I no longer have my wants; they are all Yours, and I am Yours.

Is it what you want, or is it what your loving Master wants that is worth your time and effort? If we claim what He wants, we can be sure our prayers are according to His will. There is no doubt that what He wants will be accomplished and will last forever; my puny, selfish wants will turn to dust after lasting only moments.

Lord, cause us to want what will last forever.

One Step

What do we expect when we ask God for direction? Do we expect to see a picture of where we will be in the future, with a neat diagram showing, in advance, every detail of how to get where God wants us to go? Do we sit and wait for a booming voice or a call on the phone from some prophet of God?

More often than not, what we hear from God is just this: "Put your foot there; take this one little step."

Immediately, we have a multitude of questions and complaints: "Why am I taking this step? Where does this lead? This makes no sense to me; it is not logical. Why can't I see farther down the road to the next appointment?"

If I could see the objective, I would take the shortest route to get there. My chosen path may be entirely wrong, causing me to miss what God wanted me to see, and do, and learn along the way; I may find that I have chosen a dead end. On the other hand, if I follow Him one step at a time, I will be on the right road at the right time.

Be at peace in your spirit when you make each step, knowing that He is your guide! We are climbing a mountain with the expert climber; He knows where the footing is solid. As you look around, you may think, "What if I fall?" You are a team climber attached securely with a life line to the Master; if you fall, He will put you back on the path. Don't be afraid to take that step! With your trust in Him, you will make it to the peak!

Inch Worm

I think I'll tell a story today about a little inch worm I noticed one day as I sat in the swing on Mom and Dad's patio. This little worm was inching his way around the rim of a big drainage saucer under a pot plant. Every so often, the little worm would raise the front part of its body and lean to the right or left, as if trying to grab hold of some new footing above him. When he never found any new footholds above, he continued around the rim, apparently unable or unwilling to go down the steep side to his right or left. At one place, there was a little twig sticking above the rim about half an inch and leading to the ground. Sometimes, when the little worm came to the twig, he would go up the twig to its end and then back down to the rim and continue around; other times, he ignored the twig all together. Around and around, the worm continued on his little narrow path on the rim of the saucer. He must have come up by way of the twig, but never once did I see him start back down the twig to reach the ground, his only way of escape. For the tiny little worm, it was a long way around the saucer, and from his perspective, he could not tell it was an endless circle.

As I sat there, I imagined what the worm might be thinking: "Sooner or later I'm going to get somewhere; there has to be an end to this road sometime. Once in a while, I find a road that goes up toward the luscious leaves hanging above me, but it ends almost as soon as it begins." He seemed to have but one thing on his mind—to find a way upward—but as hard as he tried, he could not find the way. The last time I saw the little inch worm, he was still going around and around in circles.

I could not get this little worm off my mind, thinking there are lessons in this worm's story. God will always show us a path to follow, but that path may not always lead in the direction we want to go. Sometimes, we have to go down before we can go up. There are times we have to just forget about the luscious leaves we saw up there in our dream world, and live the life that is in front of us. Our Lord has prepared something better for us down the road. Don't spend your life going around and around, trying to obtain things that are not obtainable.

The generation of Israelites that came out of Egypt was doomed to wander in the wilderness because of a lack of faith. They were unwilling to go down into battle with giants in order to go up into a land of milk and honey. Don't get stuck in the path of pride that refuses to go down the humble path of obedience. This is what happened to King Saul; he wasted the latter part of his life going around and around, trying to do things his own way, without God's anointing. Our own way leads us around and around to an endless nowhere.

> There is a way that seems right to a man, but its end is the way of death. (Prov. 16:25)

> Lead me, O LORD, in Your righteousness because of my enemies; make Your way straight before my face. (Ps. 5:8)

> The humble He guides in justice, and the humble He teaches His way. All the paths of the LORD are mercy and truth, to such as keep His covenant and His testimonies. (Ps. 25:9-10)

Embrace God's Provision

All that glitters is not gold; in fact, things of greatest value may not glitter at all. All the world's riches are worthless when compared to the provision of our heavenly Father.

To embrace God's provision, we must first believe that He has provision for us, whatever our need may be. "And my God shall supply all your need according to His riches in glory by Christ Jesus" (Phil. 4:19).

God's provision does not start with what men see as valuable, but with what men may consider as being of little value. Indeed, He may take nothing at all and make it enough; the need may be huge, but God's provision will always fill it to full measure.

The abundance we seek is often a big bank account or whatever else we think we need, with plenty of extra for a rainy day. Do you dream of that million-dollar prize, or that great windfall, or that most marvelous man or woman, or that grand job, or the perfect dream house? Maybe you just expect every expense, no matter how large, to be always paid in full. We like to start with the most valuable, the best, or most beautiful, and live out of that bounty. We look at provision from the top down, with great abundance that we control and can distribute where and when we see the need.

Our perception of what is needed may be very different than what God knows we need. He starts from the bottom up and builds under our feet a foundation of perfect provision, which by definition is an abundant provision, though not based on worldly riches. God's consistently perfect provision is always on time according to His plans, not ours.

Embrace His provision; love His provision, for it is exactly what you need, even if it is not grand by men's standards. When you begin to lust for more than what you have and dream of the great and wonderful things that you could have, talk to God about it and look at what the Word

says about it. Embrace that which God has put in your hands.
The work God has given you now serves a purpose for His
Kingdom and for your good. Embrace your place in God's
plan today, whether by the world's standards it is rich or
poor.

As recorded in the Bible, Joseph was sold as a slave; then,
because he was falsely accused, he was put in prison. Yet,
later God provided a promotion for him to prime minister of
Egypt. God has a plan and God has a provision; when we
seek things beyond what He gives, we cause ourselves great
distress and may even fall into terrible sin.

I believe the most important application for this teaching
is for marriages. Husband, your wife is the most spectacular
provision that God has given you other than His blood that
covered your sins. Embrace her; she is the ideal woman for
you. Wife, embrace your husband and honor him, for he is
God's gift to you. Do not even let your mind dream of
another; you will realize you already have the best if you will
only let the Holy Spirit open your heart to love the one that is
beside you.

May your fountain be blessed, and may you rejoice in the
wife of your youth. A loving doe, a graceful deer— may
her breasts satisfy you always, may you ever be captivated
by her love. (Prov. 5:18-19 NIV)

Not that I speak in respect of want: for I have learned, in
whatsoever state I am, therewith to be content. I know
both how to be abased, and I know how to abound: every
where and in all things I am instructed both to be full and
to be hungry, both to abound and to suffer need. I can do
all things through Christ which strengtheneth me. (Phil.
4:11-13 KJV)

Keep your lives free from the love of money and be
content with what you have, because God has said, "Never
will I leave you; never will I forsake you." (Heb. 13:5 NIV)

The Way of the Cross

When given his own choice, man will almost always choose the way of the crown and not the way of the cross, but only those who choose the way of the cross will ultimately keep their crown.

Moses joined with his people and became a fugitive for forty years on the backside of the desert before leading them out of Egypt. Why did God not allow Moses to become king of Egypt in order to free the Israelite slaves? I believe there are two reasons: First, it must be clearly God, not man, who is seen to accomplish the great task. Second, in this life God is not in the business of crowning kings, but training them. All God's people will one day be kings as He has promised, but first we must follow Jesus' example and carry our own cross, whatever that cross may be.

I think of Joseph who was put in a pit, sold as a slave, and made a prisoner in the prison house before he was the ruler.

Then I think of David who was a shepherd, a fool before the Philistine king, and a fugitive in the wilderness before he was the king of Israel.

Most of us will spend this life as a king-in-training, but that does not mean we must give up hope and accept the role of a slave to the struggles of life. In a dream, Joseph was shown where he was going long before it came to pass. God sent Samuel to anoint David to be king years before he felt the crown upon his head. Like Joseph and David, we can know where we are going and act accordingly. God is training us, not destroying us, as the enemy of our souls would like for us to believe.

The Lord will provide what we need when we need it; He will bring His reward to us when He knows we are ready, and not before. He is never too early, but best of all, He is never too late.

Only God Does All Things Well

We do not dare to classify or compare ourselves with some who commend themselves. When they measure themselves by themselves and compare themselves with themselves, they are not wise. We, however, will not boast beyond proper limits, but will confine our boasting to the field God has assigned to us, a field that reaches even to you. (2 Cor. 10:12-13 NIV)

Did you ever feel just a little bit of pride when you did something really well? You may have said to yourself, "I surely did well, didn't I!" Are you comparing the person you are now with the person you used to be, or are you comparing yourself with another person? Neither way is very wise, because Jesus is the standard of perfection. *Lord, help me to always have a proper perspective of who I really am, and most of all, who You are.*

Maybe you are doing really well in your endeavors in life; I truly hope and pray you are. The good that comes from our lives is what is done by the Spirit of God. In looking back at sixty years of living, and forty-nine years of following God, I see that it was only the times I listened to the Spirit and simply obeyed what He told me that anything great emerged.

What has God assigned to you? Live it, say it, build it, and walk it just as He tells you. Nobody in the world may notice, but someday you will look back and see that God did his work through you, and you will hear Him say, "Well done." Only God does all things well! Whatever He is doing in your life, you can be sure it will be done well! It appears that at the present God has assigned to me a field that reaches even to you; I pray that my words will bless, encourage, and motivate you.

Keep Your Eyes on Him

Elijah told Elisha that if he saw him when the Lord took him away, then he would have the double portion of his spirit he requested. Why was Elisha, the prophet-in-training, promised this great blessing from Elijah, his master? There is a lesson in this story that we all need to learn. Consider what Elisha had to ignore to be able to see Elijah taken away. A chariot of fire pulled by horses of fire went between them, but Elisha did not take his eyes off Elijah; he saw him as he went up by a whirlwind into heaven, and just as promised, received the double portion. We also can receive our double portion from the Lord by keeping our eyes on Him, even when there are multitudes of distractions all around us demanding our time, our thoughts, and our energy. A servant watches his master and acts in obedience to the slightest gesture of his hands. Keep your eyes on Jesus; know how to please Him by watching Him.

What did you see Jesus do today? Do likewise! It is God's plan for us to be imitators of His Son, not as an actor would imitate a character, but as an apprentice carpenter would imitate the master builder, striving to learn to do everything just as he has seen his teacher do it. Do you think the apprentice builds a building using his own interpretation of the master's methods? No, he watches and duplicates every detail of the master's craftsmanship. The apprentice does not work with the craftsman only occasionally and study his plans only once in a while; he works side by side with him day after day.

We cannot live a life like Jesus unless we watch Him work, ask him questions, listen to his instruction, and read carefully the blueprint He has written for life. He is the Master builder; we are apprentices, ever learning from our Teacher. If we take our eyes off Him, we lose that double portion of the Spirit of God that makes us like Him; we become only impersonators, not apprentices.

Jonathan and David

I have often wondered about this good man Jonathan. He seemed to be a much nobler man than most of the Kings of Israel or Judah. He did what was right, even if it meant his own hurt. He gave David his armor and sword, and even gave David the kingdom that was to come to him (see I Sam. 23:17). He was, from all we see in the Bible, a righteous and upright man. I think that Jonathan's relationship with God compares to that of most true Christians; they are good people that seek God and do not lay up treasure on earth. David, however, went a step closer to God; he was a man after God's own heart. It is good for me to be like Jonathan, but it is better for me to be like David. Jonathan's name means *Jehovah has given*. Truly, God has given us life everlasting. David's name means *loving*. It is important to God that we be lovers of Him. Jonathan's heart was right, but David was seeking to satisfy God's heart. *Lord, let me be a David!*

How can we be like David? What brings us to the place that, above all, we desire to satisfy the heart of God? This is the never-ending quest throughout our pilgrimage on earth. The most important aspect of this quest is to spend quality time with the King, listen to Him, praise Him, talk to Him, and read His Word. Pleasing God is more about being in an intimate fellowship of faith with the Savior than about doing anything. I am not saying that you shouldn't do the work of the Kingdom, but as you do the work of the Lord, let the thrust of your efforts be to know Him in an intimate way and to remain in His presence. It is a feeble work that originates from duty or guilt; it is a powerful work that pours forth out of love.

> "I have found David son of Jesse a man after my own heart; he will do everything I want him to do." (Acts 13:22 NIV)

Living Sacrifice

> Therefore, I urge you, brothers, in view of God's mercy, to
> offer your bodies as living sacrifices, holy and pleasing to
> God—this is your spiritual act of worship. (Rom. 12:1
> NIV)

What does it mean to offer our bodies as a living sacrifice,
as we are urged to do in Romans 12:1? I believe we can find
some insight into that question from the three preceding
verses in Romans 11 and from Leviticus 1:3-13.

First of all, we are not *commanded* to offer our bodies as a
living sacrifice. The verse above says *I urge you*; the word *urge*
can also be translated *beseech* or *appeal*. We must above all be
willing to be that living sacrifice.

Let us compare this sacrifice with what I consider to be
the Old Testament equivalent: the *burnt offering*. A burnt
offering was commanded to be made by the priest each
morning and each evening, once more on the Sabbath, and in
special circumstances. Also, a burnt offering could be a free-
will offering to God, which is the type of offering I will be
referring to here. The man would bring his sacrifice to the
priest, place his hand on its head, and kill it. The priest would
collect the blood and sprinkle it around the altar and by the
door of the tabernacle. Then, the man would skin the animal
and cut it in pieces. The priest would then lay the head and
fat of the animal on the altar to be burned. The man would
wash the entrails and legs clean with water; then, the priest
would burn them on the altar. Scripture says it was a
"...sweet aroma to the LORD" (Lev. 1:9). Many people
believe this was a type of the perfect Christ as He offered
Himself up to the Father. I also see the burnt offering as an
example of what happens to those who truly offer themselves
as a living sacrifice to the Lord.

First, we offer our will (head, representing our minds) on the altar and let His will become our desire. We lay down our own understanding, and by faith walk in His.

Second, we offer all we have stored up in this life (fat, representing money & possessions) on the altar. Because God already owns everything, we trust Him completely to provide for us, just as He promised.

Third, we get dirty—really dirty—and wash the entrails, (guts, representing all our hopes, dreams, expectations, desires, and longings) cleansing them by the water of the Word and putting them on the altar. God will not do this part; we have to do it willingly, not trying to hide anything of ourselves from Him.

The fourth step in offering this living sacrifice may be the hardest. We are to put our physical strengths and abilities (represented by legs) on the altar. We want to have a back-up plan; if we don't see God moving, we tend to want to go back to doing things in our own strength. Burn it up!—Burn it all up! Only the skin is left, and we are not even allowed to keep that; we give it to the priest (preacher), because there is nothing left to conceal. We leave ourselves exposed, transparent, tender, and teachable. We are no longer our own, but His. We have laid on the altar our will (mind), goods (money), desires (dreams), and physical strength (ability). We are no longer separated from Him, but consecrated unto Him, and He covers us with His protection.

Now may the God of peace Himself sanctify you completely; and may your whole spirit, soul, and body be preserved blameless at the coming of our Lord Jesus Christ. (1 Thess. 5:23)

To Reach the Lost

It is not new ways of reaching the lost that we need; it is a new heart and a burning hunger to reach the lost. If the desire is not there, all the good methods in the world will make no difference. I am not sure we really care that much about the lost. We have become too comfortable in our little world that we have built around ourselves. It is easier to just leave them where they are; that way, we don't have to get our hands dirty with their problems. We are too busy with our lives to take time to reach out to the unsaved. We are more interested in satisfying our own desires than satisfying the desire of God's heart to reach the world.

There must be a change of heart and mind. The trouble is that I don't know if we want to change; it is too easy to stay where we are, secure in our little group, doing things the way we have always done them. We first must have a desire to change; then, the willingness to let the Holy Spirit work that change into our lives. Most of us stop with a shallow desire that doesn't reach to that deep place in our heart that brings about real change. We just want what blessings God has for us, and don't care much about what blessing God would have for others.

I did not see these things in the hearts of others; I saw them in my own heart. If you will examine your hearts honestly, I suspect some of you may find yours to be similar to mine.

How do we become that channel for God's abundant grace that will reach the hearts and minds of the lost? I am not sure I have the answer. Though the answer for me may be different than the answer for you, I know God has a plan for each of us, if we will set our hearts to find it. I pray we all become channels of God's grace to that little part of the world we inhabit.

11
Grow in Integrity
✞

Let the words of my mouth and the meditation of
my heart be acceptable in Your sight, O LORD,
my strength and my Redeemer.
(Psalms 19:14)

Don't let your struggles die as struggles;
Let them bring new life,
Refreshing and encouraging others.

Rights

But as many as received Him, to them He gave the right to become children of God, to those who believe in His name. (John 1:12)

What rights do Christians have? I only find *one right* in the Bible. We have the right to become the children of God, if we receive Him and believe in Him. We like to claim all sorts of privileges as God's children, but anything that does not stem from this one right is not ours to claim. Do we have the right to our daily provisions? Do we have the right to freedom, to health, to peace? Do we have the right to have a family and a home? Yes, we have a right to all these things, but only when they are subservient to the *one right* to be children of God.

Our elder brother, Jesus, had a right to all these things as He walked upon the earth; He knew a time would come to claim all His rights as the Son of God, but His first priority was to fulfill the will of His Father.

We are quick to claim all sorts of rights for ourselves, but not so quick to claim the responsibilities. Too many of us are still ruled by one of the first words we learned as children: *mine.* We claim my rights, my things, my choices; the list goes on and on. When I die, nothing is *mine* anymore; that is why I must die with Him that I may live with Him.

Now if we died with Christ, we believe that we shall also live with Him. (Rom. 6:8)

Just Words?

Are your words spoken thoughtlessly? Do your words line up with God's Word, or do they fall in line with how you feel at the moment? Are your words ripping holes in your faith? Are your words driving a wedge between you and your brother? "Even so the tongue is a little member and boasts great things. See how great a forest a little fire kindles!" (James 3:5). Discipline those delinquent words, and demand that they march in formation with your faith in the Word of God.

Let me illustrate the power of words. Think of yourself in an army marching to war, and answer these questions: Would your general be pleased if his troops were to sing of how quickly they would be defeated and fall in the field of battle? Would this army hasten its own doom with such words? On the other hand, would your general be pleased if the soldiers were to sing of the great wisdom of their leader and of how sure they were of ultimate victory? Of which army do you want to be part?

Words alone cannot win the battle, but the wrong words can surely make defeat more likely. Words can be either comrades or foes of faith, hope, love, and truth; let the words of your mouth be true words, full of faith, hope, and most of all, love.

> Let the words of my mouth and the meditation of my heart be acceptable in Your sight, O LORD, my strength and my Redeemer. (Ps. 19:14)

One Thing

Many times I have felt like my life was going in three directions. I wanted to follow God with all my heart, but for me to get to the place where I felt fully alive in the Lord seemed to take great quantities of time. In addition, my responsibilities to my family to be industrious and make a living to provide the necessary material things in life seemed to compete with my time with God; I did not seem to be able to focus fully on both at the same time. Then, there was the desire to have something to look forward to every day, things I enjoy, the little pleasures in life which have taken different forms at different times.

Chapter one of Psalms has caused me to see clearly that my focus needs to be on *one thing*, not two or three. I am here for one purpose and that purpose revolves around my Lord.

It is the enemy of the soul that tries to divide and conquer families, friends, and churches. The way he accomplishes that is through each of us individually, by the diversion of our purpose, dividing our lives into seemingly competing parts. There is only one purpose to live for, one main thing to focus on, and that is God's purpose. I have found myself holding tightly to so many things that have no value to my real purpose, not realizing that those same things are not only keeping me from God purpose, but are also separating me from the fruit and the success He wants to bring in my life.

Do you want to be one of those of whom it is said, "Whatever he does shall prosper"?

> But his delight is in the law of the LORD, and in His law he meditates day and night. He shall be like a tree planted by the rivers of water, that brings forth its fruit in its season, whose leaf also shall not wither; and whatever he does shall prosper. (Ps. 1:2-3)

A Capital Offense

A desire to look good to others at any cost can lead us down the road to destruction. Ananias and Sapphira lied to make themselves appear to be doing more than they really were. A simple little white lie, you might say, but a capital offense in the eyes of God.

Be honest and transparent before the world. There is nothing lasting or eternal to gain by our deceits, lies, and ruses to make ourselves look good; there is everything to lose, ultimately, our lives and our souls. We lose our intimacy with God and the church when we refuse to be open and honest. (See Acts 5:1-11)

> I had rather be an honest fool,
> Loved by God,
> Than be the world's most well-thought-of liar.
>
> Our lies are not always words;
> Our deeds can lie as well,
> And both can lead us to hell.

Do not lie to each other, since you have taken off your old self with its practices and have put on the new self, which is being renewed in knowledge in the image of its Creator. (Col. 3:9-10 NIV)

Senses

Senses—do they have a reason to be?
The radiance of colors to the eye,
The splendor of the song to the ear,
The fragrance, the taste, and the touch—
God has blessed our bodies with all of these wonderful gifts.

Sights that stir the mind's desire for a thrill,
Sounds that propel the body into action,
Fragrance that draws us, as if by a cable, to its source,
Sweet tastes that create a desire for more,
Pleasing sensations that soothe the body—
Is that all there is to life, only what we can enjoy?
As from a storm or fire,
We run from all that would offend our senses.

There was a Man
Who did not turn away His eyes from our sin.
He heard such hateful sounds of scorn;
He smelled the rottenness of sin;
He tasted its revolting bitterness;
Yet, He did not seek to avoid the pain.

This Man changed the world
Because He chose to deny His senses,
And instead, please His Father.
For you, for me, for all of us
He was nailed to a cross;
To save mankind was His choice.

Senses—will you let them rule?
Will you let Him rule you and them?
Senses, given by God—
Wonderful gifts when used to please Him.

A Grain of Sand

As I stood in church today and watched while many sang and worshipped God, I did not feel worship within me. I prayed, *"Lord, I want to worship You."* I stood going though the motions of worship, but on the inside thinking of myself and my own little world.

Then God began to answer my prayer. I imagined myself growing smaller and smaller, as if a very strong telescopic lens was zooming out to see the bigger picture. I was left as only a grain of sand on a beautiful white beach. Then the Master began to walk down the beach; I could see the prints of His bare feet in the sand. He walked over me and I could see myself as a grain of sand in His footprint. Then He stopped and scooped up in His hand that footprint of sand with me in it. He put that handful of sand into a ladle over the fire, stuck His glass-maker's blowpipe into that melted blob of sand, lifted it up, and began to blow the breath of God into the molten sand. When He had finished, He held in His hand a beautiful, crystal-clear glass vessel with a handle and a pouring spout. Into His vessel, He poured transparent, golden oil that looked very beautiful as the light glowed through it.

Then the scene changed. The vessel grew larger and larger, and He began to pour oil out of the vessel upon all the earth. The vessel was the church (and each of us a part), and the oil was the working of the Holy Spirit poured out by the Master's hand through His church upon the world.

When we look at ourselves and realize we are just a grain of sand in the Master's hand, it is then that He can use us by His power to do in this world what no man or group of men can do on their own. *Oh! To be a grain of sand in His hand is my desire.*

Authority

Authority is something that many of us would like to have. Too often, though, our desire for authority is for very selfish reasons. We may want to control people and circumstances around us because we think we have the answers that others don't, or worse, because we want to elevate ourselves to a position above others.

God has given us the ability to recognize authority when we see it; however, many people don't really know what gives a person authority. Is strength, or wisdom, or great wealth the source of authority? The answer is no. Authority comes by submission. When you think about it, you realize that all the people who represent authority are able to do so because they are acting in submission to a higher authority; otherwise they would have no right to act. Do we obey the policeman because he wears a uniform, or because of the government he represents? By wearing his uniform, he shows his submission to a higher authority.

We Christians may claim authority that God has promised us in His Word, but over and over, we find ourselves unable to truly exercise it. The problem is that the chain of authority becomes broken when we are not completely submitted to God, the source of all authority.

"To him who overcomes and does my will to the end, I will give authority over the nations—." (Rev. 2:26 NIV)

"If you abide in Me, and My words abide in you, you will ask what you desire, and it shall be done for you." (John 15:7)

Lost in the Jungle of Life

Lord, I am lost in the jungle of life! Guide me back to You. I thought I knew the answers; I thought I was wise, but I am only wise enough to get lost in the midst of the tangle. It is hard to admit to myself how foolish I really am without You (my compass) and Your Word (my map) to guide me.

I strike out on my own, and it is not until I fall into a jungle swamp that I stop and seek direction. I keep getting lost in this dark forest of life with big, problem monsters nipping at my heels. It seems the choice food of these ugly monsters is my peace, though they would also quickly eat up all my time if given half a chance. Every way I turn, I see this big, grizzly mouth full of teeth waiting to bite off another chunk of me.

Lord, I keep trying and trying. How can I quit trying, but yet never give up? I know You have cut a trail through this jungle before me. You are the master Navigator of this jungle and You know every path. In this steaming jungle, I get so hot and drenched with sweat I have trouble seeing my compass and map. I know that not every day is going to be easy; struggles will always be there, for they are part of life. Though I will sometimes fail, I will never give up. *Oh, Holy Spirit, be that compass in my life and keep my eyes directed to the map of the Word.*

If I walk in the Spirit, I don't have to fear how bad the path looks or how hard it is to travel. It is the slashing of my own trail through life's tangled maze that I do not want to try again. It is not the striving that I fear; what brings dread to my soul is cutting a trail to nowhere and finding nothing there. This I know: if my eyes are on the Lord, His hand guides me along whatever dark trail I may travel. *Sweet Holy Spirit, if You are the guide, then I can bear the wilderness when I come to it.*

Into Death

Or do you not know that as many of us as were baptized into Christ Jesus were baptized into His death? Therefore we were buried with Him through baptism into death, that just as Christ was raised from the dead by the glory of the Father, even so we also should walk in newness of life. (Rom. 6:3-4)

"Baptized into His death"?
Death takes everything;
There is nothing left;
It wipes the slate clean.
Possessions are gone;
Plans and things hoped for are gone;
Faults also are gone.

Jesus arose from the dead
By the glory of the Father.
We walk in newness of life
Because of the death and resurrection of the Son.
There is a certainty of this resurrection;
There is no doubt!
If we die, we shall rise.
Refuse to die to sin, and you won't rise with Him;
Letting go is gaining.

Our Lord yearned for us, His beloved.
His love drew Him to taste this terrible death,
That He might receive His bride into His arms.
Fear not the death;
His arms are open wide for you.
The terror that we have most to fear
Is the life without God.

Contentment

I prayed this morning for contentment. Walking in the garden and feeling the sand between my toes, looking at the flowers (beautiful multi-colored irises), and listening as the birds sang in the trees, I began to feel contented, so thankful for life, peace and beauty.

I am trying to define in my mind what contentment really is, not just the dictionary definition, but what it really is to me. Do I miss contentment altogether by rushing about to accumulate things for myself or experience some pleasure that brings temporary joy. Is joy contentment? I think not, at least not what our modern culture considers joy. Deep contentment is joy not just on the surface, but an inner serenity. Though my busyness can often be a hindrance to contentment, so can fear of losing what is pleasant to me.

Contentment seems so hard to hold on to; like a beautiful butterfly, it always seems to wiggle free and fly away just out of my reach. How can I keep it? Can I control contentment, or is it just flying about as it pleases, occasionally within my reach, then eluding me as I try to catch it?

I remember these words of Apostle Paul: "I have learned to be content." Contentment is a close kinsman of faith. Solid rock faith comes by trusting in God and knowing who I am in Him. I cannot gather enough possessions, and I cannot experience enough pleasures to be satisfied. I am content because I know that everything is in His hands and I belong to Him.

Lord, I pray this prayer: *Let me learn contentment and live all my life in the shelter of Your arms. Let me stay with You, and there I will be content.*

Blessings from Struggles

How often I have asked myself, "Why must I always struggle; why can't things be easy?" Without struggle, there is no victory; without victory, there is no progress; without progress, there is only stagnation.

I am reminded of frozen waters that begin as snow on the mountain top. As the snow melts, these waters go through great struggles in their relentless effort to reach the sea. They beat against the rocks and fall from great heights in waterfalls. They are whipped and churned in the rapids. They wrestle their way through the canyons and deep gorges. They cross great deserts. Sadly, they are also polluted along their way by man's refuse. However, without these struggles they would be like glaciers frozen for millennia, never doing any good for anyone.

In the struggle to reach the sea, these waters inspire men with their beautiful falls and rapids. The cool, mountain streams bring a refreshing drink to those who are thirsty. Their unrelenting battle through the canyons brings beauty to the landscape. Even the wandering stream in the desert brings refreshing and life to plants and animals along the way.

I once saw a documentary about the Colorado River and its nearly fifteen-hundred-mile course across the west. Its waters start for the sea, but only in very wet years do they ever reach the sea. The river water is used up for irrigation of farm land and drinking water for people of nearby cities. Though you might say this great river is a failure in its quest for the sea, its struggles are not in vain. By its waters, millions are refreshed.

Don't let your struggles die as struggles;
Let them bring new life,
Refreshing and encouraging others.

Song of a Fool or Sound of Victory

As Noah built the ark those many days, he heard the ridicule of men who said, "Your hammer sings the song of a fool," but in his heart, he heard the sound of victory.

As Jonathan climbed the hill that day the army of Philistines shouted, "Come up to us, and your sword will sing the song of a fool," but before that day had passed, the Philistines lay silent upon the ground, while all Israel heard the sound of victory. (See I Sam. 14:11-14)

As young David stood his ground alone, the giant called down, "Sing your song of a fool, and I'll feed you to the birds," but at the release of his sling, the sound of victory rang out as the giant fell to the ground.

As the one called the Son of Man hung upon the cross, the Devil and his demons sang their song of triumph, and men looked up to the cross and said, "He sang the song of a fool and died." What they could not hear that day was the roaring sound of victory throughout the universe, as the keys of death, hell, and the grave were seized by that nail-scarred hand of the risen Christ. Now, you and I can sing what to the world is the song of a fool, but to the redeemed is the song of victory.

Sometimes we shrink back in fear from what would make us look foolish to those around us, when we know in the depth of our hearts we have heard the voice of God. Those who are afraid to sing the song of a fool (in the world's eyes) will never hear the sound of victory. Let our lives echo that sound that has thundered down through the ages, which is to men the song of a fool, but to God the sound of victory.

Fortress of Defense, Prison of Fear

With its thick walls and deep moat, the castle fortress that I have built around me has defended me well for many years, so well that I have lived my whole life within its walls. Going outside has seemed almost unthinkable. However, this fort has become my prison and I now find that I cannot get out of its high walls. All the many defenses I have built to keep the enemy of my fears out have become the guards to keep me in. The strong gates I have constructed to hold off the giants (of my imagination) have become the locks to my prison house. Why I did not see this before, I cannot understand. And why, now that I see it, can I not with the same hands that have built it, tear it down? The will is there, but I cannot make my hands do the work. Oh soul, why are you thus trapped in this cage of your own making? Is there no means of tearing it down level with the ground?

I plead with my God for an answer to my dilemma. The answer He gives brings dread to my soul: *"Call on the enemy for help."* Anyone can see that this would seem a foolhardy answer if the enemy is indeed an enemy. Then it becomes clear to me that in my fear I have made all men my enemies, even those good souls who would be my dearest friends; I have locked them out, for fear that they would see the nakedness of my soul and thus hate me. So I set my mind to reach out, but each time I opened my mouth to speak, one of my well-worn defenses would fill it with reasons why I could not let others into my castle. It was my place; it was my secret haven; no one must know who I really am and what I really feel. I must put on the mask, please everyone, and give them what they expect of me.

Who am I, really? What are my goals and dreams? As I pondered these things, I began to see what my goals and dreams really are; they are not part of the walls that keep others out, formed and fitted to their expectations. I am not a loner, proud of my own strength alone, for that is part of what has built this wretched wall, which began when a shy and lonely child did not fit in, so he shut everyone out behind a wall of his own fear of not being accepted.

Now I reach out again. I need a friend to help me tear down the prison wall; I have denied its existence far too long. What has been built in a lifetime may not come down in a day, but this is the day to begin to become all that God wants me to be.

These are not the ravings of a mad man, nor the scribbles of a fool, but the cry of a heart; I am sure that many hearts cry thus. If it is so with you, seek a friend to whom God would point you. He will do for you as He did for Jacob in that dreaded meeting with his brother, Esau, whom he feared because of the wrong that he had done to him. God gave Jacob favor with his brother, and he will give you favor, as well.

But Esau ran to meet him, and embraced him, and fell on his neck and kissed him, and they wept. (Gen 33:4)

Let all walls be torn level with the ground, and let there be no defense around me but the love of God.

The Feast of Fasting

Long ago there lived a mighty king who ruled a vast domain. The king was very old and had no heir to the throne.

On a beautiful spring day, the king sent out a message to all his nobles to gather for a week of feasting. And so it was, that as all the nobles gathered around his table, there was a great, sumptuous feast set before them.

While all eyes looked to the king for the signal to begin eating, he stood to his feet and made a motion to a servant in the back of the great hall. In came a beggar dressed in rags; he stood before the king, who placed in his hands a huge platter of ham. The man bowed to the king and marched out of the hall. The king then took his seat as all the lords and ladies looked on at this strange sight, wondering what it could mean. Then, the king motioned again, and in came another beggar in rags and stood before Lord Proudtower. As all eyes turned to Lord Proudtower to see what he would do, the nobleman's face turned red as he gazed at the delectable platter of roast beef that he so loved to eat. Reluctantly, he placed it in the hands of the beggar. In came the next beggar and stood before Lady Builtmore, whose favorite pumpkin pie sat on the table before her; she placed the pie grudgingly in the beggar's hands. And so it went, with each lord and lady giving to a beggar until the banquet table was bare.

Then the king arose and made a proclamation: "I declare this week *The Feast of Fasting*," after which he sat down in silence.

The banquet hall had been very quiet for much too long when the Lord Merriment stood and said, "If it please the king, let the jesters be called."

"Let it be so," said the king.

In came the jesters, not dressed in their usual brightly-colored clothes and funny hats, but with dirt smeared on their faces and dressed in rags. As they circled the hall, they performed a mime of those who were poor and sad in the kingdom. The jesters brought no laughter or joy to the lords and ladies, and many were very discomforted by the whole scene. Alas, the jesters finished their sad play and departed.

Then Lord Tunester arose and said, "If it please the king, let the singers be summoned."

The king gave his approval, and in came a ragged group, singing mournful songs of the sad and destitute and ballads about those in great distress.

So the evening went, and as the hour grew late, the king arose, bid his guests good night, and asked for their attendance at a feast the next night. As the nobles filed out into the courtyard, their grumbles grew louder; some said the old king had gone mad in his old age.

However, young Lord Humbledale said to the grumbling lords and ladies, "Why are you so upset? Has our king not been a good king these many years? Do we serve him only for what he gives us, or because of who he is?"

And so it was, that all the nobles gathered in the king's great hall the second night. To their utter displeasure, the feast became a fast just as the night before, and each was asked to return the next night.

As they gathered on the third night, the crowd of nobles was much reduced; again the feast became a fast which continued to the end of the week, with fewer in attendance each night, until on the last night only Lord Humbledale and Lady Grace sat with the king at the great feast.

This time things did not happen as in the previous days. The king arose and clapped his hands. In came the former beggars, dressed in royal clothes, each taking his seat at the king's table. The king then gave orders to his royal guard to do as they had been instructed, and they went to carry out the king's commands. Those at the table enjoyed a great feast, listened to joyous singing, and watched the court jesters stage a beautiful play. After everyone had finished eating and was well satisfied, the royal guards returned, each with a prisoner in chains, who only days before had been a noble at this same table.

Next, there was a great sound of a trumpet. The king stood to his feet, approached Lord Humbledale, and placed a crown upon his head as he made this proclamation: "You, Lord Humbledale are now crown prince of the kingdom, heir to the throne. These seated at the table are now noblemen and noblewomen of the kingdom. The last shall be first, and the first shall be last."

To Feast, or to Fast—
Will You Be First, or Last?

What do you grasp?
Will it really last?

Jesus said to them, "I tell you the truth, at the renewal of all things, when the Son of Man sits on his glorious throne, you who have followed me will also sit on twelve thrones, judging the twelve tribes of Israel. And everyone who has left houses or brothers or sisters or father or mother or children or fields for my sake will receive a hundred times as much and will inherit eternal life. But many who are first will be last, and many who are last will be first." (Matt. 19:28-30 NIV)

12
Jesus Is Coming
✝

"Behold, I am coming soon!
My reward is with me,
and I will give to everyone
according to what he has done."
(Revelation 22:12 NIV)

Today you may choose to be His own;
Tomorrow without Him, you are truly alone.

In God's Time

Knowing this first: that scoffers will come in the last days, walking according to their own lusts, and saying, "Where is the promise of His coming? For since the fathers fell asleep, all things continue as they were from the beginning of creation." For this they willfully forget: that by the word of God the heavens were of old, and the earth standing out of water and in the water, by which the world that then existed perished, being flooded with water. But the heavens and the earth which are now preserved by the same word, are reserved for fire until the day of judgment and perdition of ungodly men. But, beloved, do not forget this one thing, that with the Lord one day is as a thousand years, and a thousand years as one day. The Lord is not slack concerning His promise, as some count slackness, but is longsuffering toward us, not willing that any should perish but that all should come to repentance. (2 Peter 3:3-9)

There are many people in this world who want to believe that we live not in the last days, but on the dawn of a great awakening, when men will be truly free to throw aside their old inhibitions and superstitions. They doubt that Jesus will return in the clouds; instead, they believe that salvation comes from man's enlightenment, a new age, a new world order. These foolish ones have made it a point to disregard the undeniable truth of God's Word; to accept it would ruin their plans to make man supreme. Nevertheless, the Word of God cannot fail. Even matter itself would fly away to nothingness, and light would become darkness if not for the Word by which the heavens were formed and the earth came into existence.

He is not in a hurry and is never late. Time does not bind or loose His hands; it is His servant, accomplishing His will. His promises will not fail; what He said is exactly what He will do. Repent, O foolish ones! You think you have plenty of time, but He who holds today also holds the end.

The world around us is like water in the sink when the stopper is pulled, spiraling ever faster down the drain. I can think of countless vile words and life styles that have, in such a short time, become acceptable in our society. Don't get caught in the deception of the world's ways; they are a whirlpool of death, pulling ever deeper, eventually drowning the deluded ones in the sewers of hell.

Keep the Faith

Christians have heard and read for two thousand years that Jesus is coming. The church has heard many prophecy teachers give their interpretations concerning His return, but where is He? Is he really coming back to planet Earth? Couldn't a non-believer easily say, "I don't believe He will ever come"? How can I know that He will return?

What does the Bible say about His return? The return of the Lord is referenced hundreds of times in the New Testament. No doubt this is an important subject.

"And this gospel of the kingdom will be preached in the whole world as a testimony to all nations, and then the end will come." (Mat 24:14 NIV)

"I tell you the truth, this generation will certainly not pass away until all these things have happened." (Matt. 24:34 NIV)

"For in the days before the flood, people were eating and drinking, marrying and giving in marriage, up to the day Noah entered the ark; and they knew nothing about what would happen until the flood came and took them all away. That is how it will be at the coming of the Son of Man." (Matt. 24:38-39 NIV)

"Therefore keep watch, because you do not know on what day your Lord will come. But understand this: If the owner of the house had known at what time of night the thief was coming, he would have kept watch and would not have let his house be broken into. So you also must be ready, because the Son of Man will come at an hour when you do not expect him." (Matt. 24:42-44 NIV)

Is your life a testimony of His kingdom? Are people today spending their days reveling in pleasures? Are you watching for Him, expecting Him? He will come for those who are watching and expecting in faith.

Even so, come Lord Jesus! I look for You and long for You!

A Reflection of America
from Ezekiel 16

Oh America! You were unwanted children of the world with no one to care for you, but God saw your distress and had pity on you. He brought you to Himself and made you as royalty in a land of plenty. He gave you the finest of everything, but what have you done with God's gracious gifts? How have you responded to His abundant love? You have prostituted your great freedom and democracy and called it tolerance, perverted your great voice and called it freedom of speech, exposed to the entire world all of your beautiful body and called it art. You have burned your children on the altars of your pleasure. With your vast wealth, you have made all sorts of things to worship, but found satisfaction in none of them.

There is no atonement for your sins, America, except blood—the blood of God's own Son. He saw you when you were in that field dying in your own blood. Will you lift up your eyes to the cross and receive atonement through the redemption Jesus provided? His blood can cleanse you and make you new.

"Remember, therefore, what you have received and heard; obey it, and repent. But if you do not wake up, I will come like a thief, and you will not know at what time I will come to you." (Rev. 3:3 NIV)

"Behold, I am coming soon! My reward is with me, and I will give to everyone according to what he has done. I am the Alpha and the Omega, the First and the Last, the Beginning and the End. Blessed are those who wash their robes, that they may have the right to the tree of life and may go through the gates into the city." (Rev. 22:12-14 NIV)

Arrival with No Rival

Bullets, bullets, fall all around!
Rockets, rockets, fall to the ground!
Stopped in mid air, they all fall down!
No power against Him who wears the crown!
The King Omnipotent comes for what's His alone;
No other has right to Earth's throne.

Soldiers, soldiers, millions abound!
Armies, armies, and kings all around!
They all collapse, dead to the ground!
They have no power when His Word does sound!
He comes to conquer and end all strife;
The King rules over death and life.

These are strange words, you may say.
These are the words of that final day.
When the King comes with His saints in glory,
All earthly armies fall dead is the true story.
If knees bowed before Him have not been found,
What will come of you, if you are still around?

Will you give your life to Him this day,
That you may ride with Him all the way?
Would you reject the One who would give you life,
That you may gain only emptiness and strife?
Today you may choose to be His own;
Tomorrow without Him, you are truly alone.

Appendix

If you are searching for God, it is my hope that this appendix will give you some simple answers to help you find Him. I encourage those who are hungry for the truth to read The Holy Bible; God is its author, and you will find Him there.

Who Is Jesus?

He is the beginning of everything;
He created all that now exists;
Into nothingness He breathed life.
When there was only darkness,
He made light to shine.
When there was only loneliness,
He was a friend.
When death was the only future,
He gave His life's blood that all may live.
Who is Jesus?
He is the Son of God.
Who loves you?
Jesus!
"For God so loved the world that he gave his one and only
Son, that whoever believes in him shall not perish but have
eternal life" (John 3:16 NIV).
Do you need life?
Come to Jesus!
"For God did not send his Son into the world to condemn
the world, but to save the world through him"
(John 3:17 NIV).
Are you condemned?
Come to Jesus!
"When Jesus spoke again to the people, he said, 'I am the
light of the world. Whoever follows me will never walk in
darkness, but will have the light of life' " (John 8:12 NIV).
Is everything dark and dreary around you?
Come to Jesus!
"Come to me, all you who are weary and burdened, and I will
give you rest" (Matt. 11:28 NIV).
Are you tired of carrying a heavy load of sadness?
Come to Jesus!

God's Salvation Plan for His Creation

Why do I have this emptiness inside?
Is there a way to fill it?

God, the maker of all that exists, created mankind for this purpose: to be in fellowship with Him. Though you may not know it, this inner emptiness is a desire for God.

The first man and woman (Adam and Eve) were in fellowship with God, but they rebelled against Him and lost that fellowship. This transgression of the human race against God, which is called sin, has continued to this day.

It has always been God's desire to renew fellowship with mankind, but He is a God of law and justice, and requires that sin be punished. Because sinful flesh can never be able to pay the penalty, God provided the only worthy substitute— His only Son—to take sin's punishment once and for all, making a way for the redemption of mankind. This Redeemer was Jesus Christ.

God's plan was that men would be reconciled to Him, and Jesus chose to be part of that plan. In order to become part of the human race, and thus be able to pay mankind's debt, Jesus was born more than 2,000 years ago as a human baby to a virgin in Bethlehem, Israel. He lived a life completely without any kind of disobedience against God; He did not sin at all. The enemies of Jesus wrongfully accused Him and had Him put to death on a cross made from timbers. He was cruelly beaten and His hands and feet were nailed to the cross; He died there willingly as a sinless sacrifice for our rebellion against God. Three days later He rose from the dead, just as He said He would. On several occasions during the days that followed, he physically appeared to His friends and talked with them. Later, He returned to heaven in a cloud to be with His Father.

We now have a way to be free from this sinful state and find new fellowship with God, through Jesus, the only way to the Father.

Jesus said to him, "I am the way, the truth, and the life. No one comes to the Father except through Me." (John 14:6 NKJV)

We must realize and accept the fact that we are in need of a savior, surrender to God, and receive the forgiveness Jesus paid for with His blood. We must leave behind our sinful past, and let God be the sole authority in our lives. He will not only give us amnesty for our rebellion, but will make us pure in heart, just as if we had never sinned. He will embrace us as part of His family—sons and daughters—children of God.

He loves us always and will give us the ability to follow Him and live by His Word. As children always do, we will sometimes make mistakes, make wrong decisions, and commit sin. He will not hold the sins of His children against them if they confess their sins to Him; He is ready and willing to forgive, and to lovingly guide them.

It is His promise that He will gather all those who belong to Him into His physical presence to live forever in joy and peace with Him.

www.ingramcontent.com/pod-product-compliance
Lightning Source LLC
Chambersburg PA
CBHW051826040426
42447CB00006B/390